"Fascinating to see wealth management being interwoven so finely with cricket - makes it very interesting and easy for the reader to acheive his financial goals."

Rahul Dravid, Former Indian Cricket Team Captian

WINNING THE WEALTH GAME

Cricket Strategies for Financial Freedom

Dr. Sanjiv Mehta

This is a work of nonfiction. The events and the incidents mentioned in the book are true and real. However, some names and characteristics have been changed, some events have been compressed, and some dialogues have been recreated.

First Edition: Tata McGraw-Hill Publishing Company Limited.
Second Edition; Story Mirror, June 2026
Printed in India

Printed at: Gapmeta Ventures Pvt. Ltd., Navi Mumbai

Typeset in EB Garamond

ISBN: 978-93-6070-974-7

Cover Design: Priya Vora

STORYMIRROR
Stories that reflect you

Publisher: StoryMirror Infotech Pvt. Ltd.
Unit No-F/705, 7th Floor, Kailas Corporate Lounge,
Veer Savarkar Road, Vikhroli Park Site,
Vikhroli West, Mumbai-400079,
Maharashtra, India.

Web: storymirror.com
Facebook: @storymirror
Twitter: @story_mirror
Instagram: @storymirror
Email: marketing@storymirror.com

To my parents, Mr. Bhagwan Baksh Mehta and Mrs. Sarswati Mehta, for the values they instilled and intense focus on their children's education.

To my wife and soulmate, Parveen, for sharing and doing everything together and for being such a loving and complete partner.

To our beautiful and bright children, Sahir and Tarini, the purpose, the future; and whose amazing idea will be my next book.

To my siblings, Naveen, Neeraj and Alka, for our shared childhood where everything was a game full of fun and joy.

Author's Note to the 2026 Reissued Edition

When Winning the Wealth Game was first published in 2007, investing was simpler—but not necessarily easier. Information was limited, choices were fewer, and yet the same fundamental question persisted: how does one build wealth with clarity, discipline, and purpose?

Nearly two decades later, the landscape has changed dramatically. Investors today are surrounded by constant information, endless options, and an always-on market environment. Decisions are faster, reactions are sharper, and distractions are everywhere. And yet, the core challenge remains unchanged—how to stay grounded, think clearly, and act with conviction over the long term.

It is for this reason that this book is being reissued exactly as it was written. The principles it is built on are not tied to a particular time, market cycle, or product—they are anchored in behaviour, judgment, and perspective. In a world that often rewards immediacy, these principles offer something quieter, but far more enduring.

This edition is being brought out for a new generation of readers—those who are beginning their journeys, as well as those who may wish to revisit the fundamentals with fresh eyes.

I remain grateful to the team at Tata McGraw Hill for their role in the original publication of this book. I also thank Story Mirror for bringing out this reissued edition and enabling these ideas to reach a wider audience today.

If this book helps you pause, reflect, and make even a few better decisions along your financial journey, it will have achieved what it set out to do.

Dr Sanjiv Mehta
May 2026

Contents

सत्यमेव जयते

डॉ. सी. रंगराजन
Dr. C. RANGARAJAN

अध्यक्ष
अध्यक्ष, प्रधानमंत्री की आर्थिक सलाहकार परिषद
विज्ञान भवन एनेक्स, हॉल 'H'
मौलाना आजाद रोड,
नई दिल्ली–110011
CHAIRMAN
Economic Advisory Council to the Prime Minister
Vigyan Bhavan Annexe, 'H' Hall
Maulana Azad Road
New Delhi-110 011

October 24, 2006.

Foreword

This is a lucidly written book on finance. Though written in a lighter vein, it conveys to the readers the essentials of finance. For lovers of cricket this book is a double bonus. They get to know more about cricket and finance. The analogies from cricket are both appropriate and telling. They make the book lively.

It is not uncommon to find people who suffer a deterioration in their lifestyle after retirement. Even individuals who have spent their whole lives in finance and economics are poor managers of their finances. Generally speaking, the level of financial literacy is low and the book on hand, fulfills an important need. The message of the book is that everyone must in their active working life pay attention to how they will manage their life after retirement. In everyone's life there are, to use the author's felicitous expression, the 'Wealth Accumulating' and the 'Wealth Harvesting' periods. This book basically tells everyone ways by which funds can be invested wisely. It takes the readers through the various characteristics of the different financial assets and advises how they should be combined to achieve a balanced portfolio of investment. All this has been done with sparkling wit and humour. Individuals must know that their financial decisions today will be important determinants of their future lives. Overall, Dr Sanjiv Mehta's *Winning the Wealth Game* will go a long way in facilitating people to live comfortably their post retirement lives. Truly, this is a great service.

(C. Rangarajan)

Preface

The message in this book is that you can generate the wealth and lifestyle you aspire, not only in the good phases of economic cycle, which we are seeing presently, but also in low phases of the cycle which inevitably follow. Moreover, you do not have to live a frugal life today, to retire comfortably tomorrow. You can spend what it takes to have a great life now and still have enough left to invest for a happy life tomorrow.

Wealth is much more than merely showing off your achievements. It represents the ability to attain the freedom to do what you want in life and to add to the advancement of our society. I attempt to show you how to attain wealth and financial freedom. It all comes down to understanding fundamental trends, both economic and personal, and basic principles of investing.

I have endeavoured to produce a practical book which focuses on most of your 'how to' questions. For example, I answer how to organize your financial information simply, read economic and personal cycles, identify your financial goals, employ various asset classes effectively, utilize insurance favorably, incorporate taxation and plan for a happy retirement. In the last chapter, I integrate everything discussed earlier to provide numerous examples of how your assets can be allocated optimally in different stages of economic and personal cycles. I hope and believe that you will find the book comprehensive and useful with the potential of becoming a lifelong companion.

However, the most sensible ideas on financial planning and the most articulately expressed thoughts on wealth creation may be wasted if they are not presented in an entertaining style. I feel that *Winning the Wealth Game* does that by taking an innovative 'cricket' approach.

Rather than flooding you with daunting charts and a series of dull and tedious numbers, *Winning the Wealth Game* will both entertain and inform you. Through the adventures and exploits of Rahul, our financial cricket hero, you will learn that sound wealth management is not only relatively simple, but can also be fun.

I wish you good reading and living in style now and in retirement.

SANJIV MEHTA
www.financedoctor.biz

Acknowledgements

The experience of writing my first book has been more rewarding than I could have imagined. Perhaps, its greatest reward comes from the help, support and encouragement of family and friends. As wealth management is so intertwined with life itself, this book has been the culmination of influences and experiences right since childhood. To all of you I owe a great debt of thanks.

My father late Mr. Bhagwan Baksh Mehta and my mother Mrs. Sarswati Mehta instilled a great love for learning in all four of us and excellent values governing our lives. They always encouraged us to practice *swadharma* - focusing and honing your gifts and putting them to use for others. This book hopefully will be of great help to many people.

My parents-in-law, Mr. Prem Bagai and Mrs. Pam Bagai were a great source of encouragement and inspiration. Their enthusiasm and abiding interest along with suggestions and feedback kept on helping the project move forward.

My sisters-in-law Irene Mehta, Renu Mehta and Poonam Bagai and my also passionate about cricket brother-in-law, Pavan Bagai (who has seen matches in all important international venues) provided very useful and unique insights. Irene and Renu even facilitated cricket in the deserts of Arabia. My nephews and nieces Siddharth, Vikram, Ian, Sakshi, Mansi, Rohan, Angad, Akram and Ashvin, being of diverse age groups and true representatives of the next generation, provided fresh perspectives on future trends.

I have been fortunate enough to have very diverse educational and work experiences and made many enduring friendships on the way. Memories of childhood cricket revolve around my next-door neighbour, Deshpal Singh Kwatra (who went on to play Ranji Trophy for Delhi) and cousins Sunil and Sanjay Baweja. We shared a deep love for the game—played, talked and watched cricket together. Dr. B. Girish Rai, a childhood friend and also a classmate through school and at the All India Institute of Medical Sciences had an equally good facility with numbers and sports—his persistent questions on how he should manage his considerable wealth helped a lot. My close friends at Wharton—Kanwar Chadha, Ravi Kumar, Rajiv Kohli and I share an enduring memory of huddling around the radio on Locust Walk in the University of Pennsylvania campus, listening to BBC commentary of India's World Cup victory in 1983. My cricket understanding increased manifold due to my numerous, although futile attempts to make Tristan Renz, another close Wharton friend, understand the difference between baseball and cricket. Those were the days before cable TV and globalization of cricket.

A special thank you goes to close friends at Hyderabad, Saudagar and Imtiaz Anwar, Subhash and Viji Naik, M. Gautam and K.V. Subramaniam for their helpful ideas and suggestions. Our artist friend, Lester Anthony Paul provided tremendous help in cover designs and various sketches.

I will also like to thank Mr. Ajay Shukla, Managing Director, McGraw-Hill Education (India) for taking tremendous personal interest in the book, Mr. Roystan La'Porte for galvanizing his publishing and marketing teams into well-directed action, Mr.

Chandra Sekhar and Mr. Souvik Mukherjee for moving the project forward.

My eldest brother Naveen, my mentor in many important decisions, is always there to help and inspire. During our childhood, he would convert everything into a tournament where we have even played competitive Ludo championship and multiple indoor versions of cricket using cards, books or dice. Neeraj, my best friend along with being a very encouraging brother, keeps on guiding with his creative inputs. He has an amazing ability to come up with very perceptive, humorous and practical insights. Alka, our only sister was a full participant in all these childhood ventures including playing cricket in diverse exciting locales of verandah, street or a park. She is a constant source of support and encouragement.

Our children Sahir and Tarini, though very young, took tremendous interest in all that was going on. Sahir's regular phone calls to ensure I reported on time for our evening cricket ritual and Tarini's curiosity about the entire process, especially as her present career objective is to be a writer, ensured that cricket and the book were never far from my mind. Their questions and discussions provided lots of zest and fun, kept energy levels high and helped put things in perspective. They really define what the future is and have quite amazingly, provided an exciting idea for my next book.

This book just would not have been possible without my wife, Parveen. She is my soulmate and a complete partner with her intense loving, caring and sharing in everything, including this book. She even researched cricket matches so that we could find the most appropriate one for various themes and her cricket knowledge has gone up manifold. Our constant discussions on every aspect since its inception made this book a wonderfully exciting project—a challenging yet joyful journey.

SANJIV MEHTA

Part 1

Introducing the Wealth Game

Courtesy: Pradeep Mandhani/imageallsports.com

Everyone can win this game: Kapil Dev lifts the World Cup after India's win, June 25, 1983

Chapter 1

Introducing the Wealth Game

Rahul leapt out of his comfortable chair and grabbed the phone, knocking off the lamp in his eagerness. This was the call Rahul had been waiting for. Raghu Malviya was on the line. He finally wanted Rahul to lead the Wealth Creation Team, which had lost yet again. It had choked on big occasions repeatedly. Raghu was livid and distressed and railing at the injustice of it all. Why was everything always dependent on him? He had to look after winning the elections, deciding TV rights, organizing new fixtures; and they expect him to be responsible for match results too. Fretting and fuming, he let off steam, while Rahul clasped the receiver with a wide grin on his face – just the key words resounding in his ears, everything else fading into a pleasant drone in the backgroun...*you are the new captain.*

Rahul was happy and enthusiastic about his new role. Iqbal's steadfastness would be his guiding light; Gurus, Raghus, Dadas notwithstanding. He was aware of the huge impact of playing this game well. Making right decisions can have a profound positive effect not only on him, but on everybody around him. The quality of life can become so much better, even explaining the broken lamp so much easier.

What excited Rahul was the fact that in this game he will be all in all - captain, strategist, team selector, coach and behavioural psychologist - for the team. He had been given a completely free hand with full decision-making power. No need to be wary of backstabbing, deal-making, petty politics; just a pure and simple result orientation.

With complete decision-making power, comes complete responsibility. The credit or discredit for the results will be wholly and solely Rahul's. He will not enjoy the luxury of a blame game. However, he knows that he just has to follow and implement some important principles to win the game. Fortunately, the opportunity has come now, when Rahul is well prepared. His mind goes back to when his learning the process of wealth creation and management had started. It was a rocking party at a friend's place.

The Party with a Wealth Theme

It was the early hours of the morning. The party was still in full swing. The music was nice and soothing. A few people were gently swaying on the dance floor. Rahul's close friend, Deven Singhani, had organized this party with wealth as the theme. The winner would be the one who could persuade the judges that he was the wealthiest among all the guests. No mean feat in this typical page-3 get-together of industrialists, actors, players, senior executives and politicians. Rahul finds the word 'wealth' fascinating. It evokes so many varying images. Different people interpret the word in their own myriad ways.

There was suddenly a hush: the judges were about to announce the winner. The party host was the hot favourite. Deven Singhani was confident of victory. After all, his palatial house, expensive cars, wife dripping diamonds, extensive conversations of exotic vacations, bore testimony to his overwhelming wealth. He was tipped to win the game. Until, some interesting contenders came up.

Dr. Rameshwari staked his claim to being the wealthiest saying he did not even remember what he owned. The judges were impressed till they asked him his wife's name and discovered that the old professor suffered from amnesia.

Tristan Benz, a BPO senior executive from USA said that he was truly wealthy since his son's homework was being outsourced to a kid in India. Some laughter, but no prizes.

Bipasha Dutta, a successful model, tried to persuade the judges by saying that she attended the swankiest parties, socialized with celebrities, lived in a luxurious apartment, travelled globally, and possessed all the good things of life. She was eliminated too. When asked how she planned sustaining this lifestyle, pat came the reply-marry a rich man.

Dr. Suresh Pai, a very successful surgeon wagered his claim saying his money creation ability literally lay in his hands. That made him a very strong contender and odds on him winning the game steadily improved.

Then the surprising results were announced. A defense services officer, Col. Ravish Gupta, was declared the winner. Among good-humored protests and fixing allegations, the judges provided some very valid reasons for their verdict.

An All-Encompassing Wealth Definition, which puts us on the Road to Wealth

The judges said that to arrive at a decision, they focused on the following definition of wealth:

A person is wealthy if his passive income is sufficient to sustain a desirable lifestyle.

They explained that passive income is the income resulting from investments, rents, royalties and similar avenues. Active income is the income earned from active employment. Wealth creation is the process of establishing a strong connection between income and wealth, and the proportion of passive income indicates how strong that connection is. It is, in a way, an attempt to reach a state of financial freedom.

The audience clamored how come the successful surgeon Dr. Pai did not make the grade. After all he had an established practice and a rich lifestyle. But the judges found that he had not created the requisite connection between income and wealth. He is a high-income, high-expense person - with his busy schedule, he never devotes much time to managing his financial resources. He is almost totally dependent on active income. With advancing age, he wants to reduce the workload but that implies compromised lifestyle. For him to feel wealthy is difficult. Passive income as a percentage of his total income is minuscule and he cannot sustain his lifestyle without working long hours.

The guests were equally surprised about Deven Singhani's exclusion. There the judges emphasized the phrase 'desirable lifestyle' in their definition of wealth. He was stumped in the last round of questioning about his idea of desirable lifestyle. Deven answered that it will be to acquire more and more things, much more than what he already has - for example, he is desperate to buy a private jet. He says that he is never satisfied with what he already has and is always looking for more, more and more. The judges decided that his present resources were insufficient to sustain his desirable lifestyle.

The Colonel, on the other hand, was well on his way to fulfilling his important, deeply cherished financial goals - comfortable retirement equivalent to his current lifestyle, children's high quality education and owning a nice, spacious house in his hometown. He easily had the greatest wealth consciousness and was the true winner.

Rahul's reverie gets disturbed by the thought that a lot of action has to be taken to translate his dream of victory into reality. He must review what the game is all about, his opponents, and the action steps he needs to take.

The Wealth Game – What is it all about?

There are two teams battling it out : the wealth creation team and the financial needs team.

Wealth Creation Team

This is Rahul's team. It has to put up as many runs as possible while taking optimal risks. It has to keep the scorecard ticking while preserving wickets. In financial terms, Rahul has to get the best out of his financial resources and make required returns while taking minimal risks.

Financial Needs Team

These are the opponents Rahul is facing. This team will try to overtake the wealth creation team's total score. Rahul, as captain, has to size up this opponent and then strategize to defeat them. He has to know the target, in order to pace his innings. In financial terms, Rahul has to identify, quantify, and prioritize his important needs and then find the best way to marshal his financial resources to meet these needs.

This is a Game Everybody is Playing

Nobody has a choice; everybody is playing this game, even if they do not realize it. Everybody has financial resources on one side and financial goals and needs on the other.

If needs are not properly identified and quantified, the individual is playing the game in a rudderless fashion, without any goals or targets.

On the resource side, if his allocation is not thought through, he is batting indiscriminately. If he is very cautious and not deploying assets in any return enhancing asset class, he will come up with a very small total. On the other hand, if he is taking indiscriminate and random risks, again the total score is very modest. In either case, he will lose this important game of life.

For example, one lakh of rupees set aside for a child's education in a fixed bank deposit at 6% will produce Rs. 2.85 lakhs when the child is 18 years of age. Same amount earning 15%, will give rise to Rs. 12.4 lakhs, thus giving solid options for the child's education. Essentially, by not optimizing your returns or taking advantage of opportunities, one is playing a losing game. Not marshalling your resources effectively will lead to unfulfilled important financial goals. On the contrary, investing effectively promotes a winning habit. If Rs. 1 lakh today can give rise to Rs. 12.4 lakhs, there will be a strong motivation to save Rs. 50,000 more and try to reach Rs. 20 lakhs.

Just being aware that we are playing the game is a big step forward. It goads us on to progress.

This is a Game where Everybody can be a Winner

What makes this game exciting is that everybody can be a winner - every person is running his own race with differing needs, resources and risk-taking capacity. It is a highly individualized, customized game. As Rahul's son would say, this wealth game is really cool – everybody is a potential winner. The model, surgeon, professor, industrialist, army officer, government employee, business executive can all win because wealth has two sides – wealth creation and financial needs. Everybody has lots of flexibility to calibrate.

It is Actionable

Passive income forces us to think about our income and expenses and how we are managing our assets and liabilities. Are we creating a connection between income and wealth and is our passive income increasing? Simultaneously, we are looking at the other side of the equation of creating a desirable lifestyle. This forces us to think of what our deeply felt and important needs are and whether these are being taken care of.

Playing this Game Well Enhances Life Considerably

However, consequences of losing this game are severe; either compromising current lifestyle or compromising deeply cherished financial goals like a comfortable retirement, children's education, and a nice home.

On the other hand, playing this game well can have a profound effect on the quality of your life. The American bestseller *The Millionaire Next Door*, written by two American professors, is the culmination of intensive research on this subject. They followed a select group of individuals for 20 years. Some members of that group became wealthy and some did not. The professors analyzed the factors underlying wealth creation and concluded that one of the most important factors is effective personal financial planning and decision-making.

In other words, people who became wealthy played the wealth game much better and that's what this book is all about — Rahul's strategy and team selection given the pitch and his opponents; his action steps for ensuring success.

Laying a solid foundation is important for winning- Warren Buffet, legendary winning investor

Courtesy: Pradeep Mandhani/imageallsports.com

Laying a solid foundation is important for winning- Imran Khan, legendary winning cricketer

Chapter 2

Similarities to Cricket

Rahul marvels at the fact that the wealth creation game has remarkable similarities to one-day cricket, although the time horizon is much longer. The feeling of exhilaration when hitting the winning shot or when getting the last wicket of the opposing team is replicated many times over when winning this game of life. He starts enumerating all the similarities in order to leverage his cricket experience.

1. Building up an Innings

The game of wealth creation is nothing but building up an innings bit by bit, run-by-run capitalizing on opportunities and preserving profits. In cricket the challenge is to score runs while not losing wickets. It's all a question of maximizing the score at minimal risk.

2. Laying a Solid Foundation

Imran Khan, after winning the 1992 World Cup, said that retaining wickets and consequent ability to accelerate was an important factor for their success. In an investment portfolio, a solid foundation is similarly important. First, liquidity has to be taken care of, then safety, and finally acceleration with yield enhancing assets.

3. Always on the Lookout for Runs - Not Letting Go of Opportunities

Australia is dominating world cricket and one of the important factors in their approach is converting dot balls into 1s, 1s into 2s and so on. They do not let go of any scoring opportunities. They are always on the lookout for weak bowlers and weak fielders. Similarly, a winning portfolio will not have funds lying idle. Even liquid and safe funds will earn returns. Capitalizing on numerous investment opportunities makes a difference.

4. Importance of Right Technique - Just Follow Basic Investment Principles

Batsmen like Tendulkar, Lara, Ponting, Jayasuriya and Gilchrist have good averages as well as good strike rates. This implies that not only do they score consistently but also at a fast rate.

The beauty of the wealth game is the same - just by following basic investment principles, it is possible to consistently make high returns.

5. Knowing Your Goals

No victory is possible if there is no well-defined target. If a team does not know what a winning total will be, it is leaving the result to chance. Similarly in the wealth game, it is important to define and quantify your financial goals like ability to maintain a good retirement lifestyle, children's education and a good home.

6. Long-Term Orientation

Victory in a one-day cricket match is not determined by scoring 18 runs in one over. It is achieved by putting up a good overall total which surpasses the opponent's total. Similarly, in the wealth creation game, many investors get sidetracked if their one stock does exceptionally well for a short period of time. However, real victory lies in converting one lakh rupees set aside for a child's education at her birth into 15 lakh rupees when she is 18 years old; thus giving her a real head start and making a real difference.

7. When to Attack, When to Defend

Each over is different. Conditions are dynamic in both cricket and the wealth game.

In some ways, each over can be compared to a year of investment life, where the challenges and results can be variable. Economic conditions are different, personal conditions might have changed and therefore, while the final goal will be still be the same, the path has to be evaluated in a dynamic way.

In a cricket match, if the target is 250 runs in 50 overs, no captain will direct his team to score 5 runs in each and every over. There will be some maiden overs while some overs will be very productive. When to attack and when to defend is an important skill determining success.

8. Reading the Pitch Well – When to Enhance and When to Preserve Hard Earned Capital

India presently is a very good pitch. It is at a high growth stage of the economic business cycle and is thus, a very attractive investment destination. Contrastingly, European economies are slow-growing. Therefore, earning less than 15% annualized return in India will be a losing proposition while trying to earn more than 15% return in Europe will be hazardous.

Rahul realizes that in a conducive environment, he has to ensure utilization of opportunities and in a difficult economic environment, he has to implement preservation strategies.

9. Assessing Team Strengths and Weaknesses — Determining Your Own Winning Total

Winning totals are individualized and customized and everybody can be a winner in the wealth game. Life cycle factors including age, sex, marital status, number of children, wealth, current income, future needs and a plethora of factors determine what an individual's winning total is. For example, an about to retire person has to create a monthly income while a young 35 year old person can take a lot more risks in order to build up a sizable corpus for later needs. Additionally, desired lifestyle will be very different from one person to another. For one team, a total of 320 could be a losing proposition while for some, a total of 150 could be a winning one.

10. Selection of Right Balanced Team - Asset Allocation

Rahul realizes that this is one of the most important decisions. There are different asset classes (players) available with different risk/return characteristics. What makes stocks and real estate the top strikers and indispensable for a winning team? How and when do we deploy them? What is the role of bonds (defensive players)? Are small savings instruments over the hill and should they be retired? Or could there be a big hue and cry if these are dropped from the team?

11. Diversification - It is a Team Sport

Harry M. Markowitz won the 1992 Nobel Prize in Economics for his diversification theory. He analyzed how wealth can be optimally invested in assets which differ in regard to their expected return and risk. Essentially, he came up with a simple idea of not putting all your eggs in one basket, since it reduces risk considerably.

The Indian team, by depending solely on Sachin, was not making it as a consistent winner. Having several good strikers made a tremendous difference to the team's fortunes. Similarly, a winning portfolio requires stocks, bonds, real estate, insurance, and other classes. Moreover, safe and liquid instruments are required too. An important factor is determining appropriate weightage to each asset class in the portfolio mix.

12. Special Rules, Regulations and Performance

Every game has its own set of rules that can be capitalized on. In the first 10 overs, the fielding team can have only two fielders on the boundary line. Therefore, the batting teams try to accumulate as many runs as possible by sending their best strikers.

In the wealth game, it is beneficial to capitalize on government regulations especially taxation. For example, long-term capital gains tax on stocks is absolutely zero and investment in ELSS (equity linked savings schemes) reduces taxable income up to a maximum of one lakh rupees under section 80C. More allocation to stocks is obvious, since the government wants to channelize domestic savings in stocks.

13. Winning Mindset - Behavioural Finance

Indian team losing in 12 of the last 13 finals was no coincidence. Choking on big occasions has a lot to do with inability to handle mental pressure. The Indian team enlisted the services of an Australian sports psychologist and it has proved to be beneficial. Yield enhancing instruments are volatile and lead to lots of investors choking too. Rahul realises that understanding behavioural finance and investor psychology will be an important determinant of his success.

14. Going Forward on this Journey

Rahul's happiest memory is that of India winning the World Cup in 1983. This happened despite the Indian team not matching the star power of West Indies. However, as a team it proved to be the best. The players with their diverse skills complemented each other and became a potent combination. The team was aware of its strengths and weaknesses and leveraged its strengths very successfully. They read the conditions very well and devised effective strategies. Above all, they had a winning mindset.

Rahul is determined to learn quickly all the skills and replicate that super success.

Scorecard

India

Batsman	how out	runs	balls	4s	6s
Uthappa	c Gayle b Powell	28	17	3	2
Ganguly	st Ramdin b Gayle	68	82	8	1
Dravid	c Simmons b Samuels	78	109	7	0
Tendulkar	not out	100	76	10	1
Dhoni	not out	40	20	1	3

Extras (in 14, w 9, nb 4) 27

Total (in 50 ovs) **341/3**

FoW: 1-47 (Uthappa, 6.3 ov), 2-148 (Ganguly, 24.6 ov), 3-266 (Dravid, 43.4 ov)

Bowling	O	M	R	W	(E)
Powell	8	0	68	1	(1nb, 1w)
DR Smith	8	0	49	0	
Emrit	9	0	65	0	(2nb, 1w)
Samuels	9	0	51	1	
Gayle	9	0	54	1	(1w)
Bradshaw	8	0	60	0	(1nb, 2w)

West Indies

Batsman	how out	runs	balls	4s	6s
Chanderpaul	c Harbbajan b Zaheer	14	23	2	0
Gayle	b Agarkar	6	11	1	0
DS Smith	c Yuvraj b Pathan	24	31	2	0
Samuels	c pathan b Kumble	55	63	7	1
Lara	run out (Pathan)	3	2	0	0
Simmons	not out	4	6	1	0
Ramdin	c Kumble b Harbhajan	40	52	5	0
DR Smith	lbw b Kumble	0	5	0	0
Emrit	c Uthappa b Agarkar	13	33	1	0
Bradshaw	not out	14	16	2	0
Powell	c sub (Raina) b Yuvraj	1	3	0	0

Extras (lb 3 w. 4) 7

Total (all out in 41.4 ovs): **181**

FoW: 1-10 (Gayle, 2.6 ov), 2-32 (Chanderpaul, 7.6 ov), 3-65 (DS Smith, 14.1 ov), 4-72 (Lara, 14.5 ov), 5-83 (Simmons, 16.4 ov), 6-148 (Samuels, 30.2 ov), 7-153 (Ramdin, 31.2 ov), 8-155 (DR Smith, 32.5 ov), 9-180 (Emrit, 40.2 ov), 10-181 (Powell, 41.4 ov)

Bowling	O	M	R	W	(E)
Agarkar	9	0	40	2	(2w)
Zaheer	6	1	21	1	
Pathan	7	0	43	1	(2w)
Harbhajan	8	1	30	1	
Kumble	7	1	27	2	
Yuvraj	4.4	0	17	1	

Result: India won by 160 runs and series 3-1

Important first step for any game: organizing information and measuring progress

Chapter 3

Scorecard-Organizing Information

Introduction

Rahul realizes that to be a winner, he has to know where his team stands now and subsequently at any given point in time. Only then the right strategy can be implemented in a dynamic environment. He wants an effective tool for measuring progress, whether his team is on a winning path, whether it is nearing its goals, and whether the current strategy requires modification.

4 Square Scorecard

Rahul zeroes in on a scorecard with four squares of income, expenses, assets and liabilities. It is simple, concise and allows him to put all his financial information in one page. He is particularly happy that this scorecard is based on individual financial statements. After all, an individual should take decisions akin to what a smart business would do to grow its balance sheet.

Income and expense squares form an income statement and show immediately his savings and whether there is potential to save more or move his expenses to an area which enhances his current lifestyle. Difference between assets and liabilities is net worth, a very popular measure of wealth and will inform him about his team's progress.

Table 3.1: 4-square scorecard

INCOME	ASSETS
EXPENSES	LIABILITIES

Income Square

The most important factor in the income square is the distinction between active income and passive income. Active income comes from employment, profession, or a business. Passive proceeds will include property rent, interest on deposits, dividends and capital gains from stocks and royalties.

Rahul intends keeping an eye on how passive income is growing in absolute terms and as a proportion of total income. This will be an important performance determinant since our wealth definition focuses on passive income.

Table 3.2: Income Square

INCOME
Active sources
employment salary
professional income
business income
Passive sources
rent from property
investment income
royalties
any other
COMBINED INCOME
Deductions
Taxation
Pension Contribution
any other
NET INCOME

Expenses Square

Rahul wants a very clear picture on what the opposition is up to. He knows that it is inevitable that he will have to concede a fair number of runs. After all, he has to maintain a good and comfortable lifestyle. However, he is aware of the opponent's ability to creep stealthily and silently. This square will remove the surprise element thus facilitating Rahul's control.

Table 3.3: Expenses Square

EXPENSES
Food
Clothing
Housing
Children related
Health & Insurance
Transportation
Appliances
Discretionary
Interest Expense
any other
TOTAL EXPENSES

Rahul has divided expenses methodically into important categories starting with *roti, kapada and makaan* (food, clothes and shelter). Then he lists children, health, and transportation expenses. Last but not least is the interest expense resulting from loans for housing, car, and other appliances, and on his credit card.

Table 3.4: Assets Square

ASSETS	
Liquidity	***6-12 mths basic expense***
	short term deposits
	liquid funds
	Total Liquidity
Safety	***current income generating***
	bonds with coupon
	saving schemes with periodic income
	real estate on rent
	short term debt funds
	monthly income plans
	long term
	provident fund
	contributory pension schemes
	small saving schemes
	real estate for own usage
	fixed term deposits
	jewellery
	Total Safety
Yield Enhancing	
	stocks - direct & equity funds
	real estate for investment
	bonds & bond funds
	pension ULIPs
	commodities
	art, antique
	structured products
	Total Yield Enhancing
TOTAL ASSETS	

Assets Square

Asset is ownership of something advantageous. It could be real estate, home, bank deposits, stocks, and mutual funds, fixed income securities, commodities, precious metals, jewellery, car, art, and so many varied things. This is the most important square and is akin to a batting square. This is where runs are made and doing well here mainly determines whether one wins the wealth match or not.

Rahul understands that while going for runs, he has to protect wickets too. Some assets have to be liquid and readily available for contingencies even if their returns are low. Some assets have to be in absolutely safe instruments like government securities that retain their value even in extremely adverse circumstances. Only after liquidity and safety have been taken care of, the remaining assets can be utilized in return-enhancing asset classes. This is what the art of asset allocation (batting) is all about and as the match develops, Rahul dwells on these aspects.

Liabilities Square

Liabilities square lists the loans, their due dates, interest rate being paid and the purpose for which the loan has been taken. It provides important information on what kind of assets being financed by loans and how much this square is contributing to total expenses. It also renders an easy comparison of interest rates being paid on different kinds of loans. Some loans like credit card loans might be carried at very high interest rates and could be eliminated easily. On the other hand, a home loan is financing an asset that can produce a rental cash flow and at the same time might show capital gains. This is the fielding square where an intelligent placement of fielders can save lots of runs.

Table 3.5: Liabilities Square

LIABILITIES

Short-term
credit card loan
borrowings on life insurance
personal loan installment
accrued income taxes
other obligations
Long-term
home loan principal yet to be repayed
loans to purchase investment assets
loans to purchase personal assets

TOTAL LIABILITIES

Interrelationship between Squares

Rahul appreciates that the four squares are not stand-alone squares; instead, they have deep connections. A good awareness of these relationships can be the difference between a winner and a loser. If his assets are producing good returns, it adds to his passive income, thus increasing the total income. This in turn increases savings, which can then be put in productive assets. For example, a good proportion invested in stocks and real estate producing high returns will increase his passive income significantly.

Contrastingly, a liability adding heavily to the expenses could erode savings thus decelerating the asset build up. For example, a credit card debt being carried at high interest rates would be detrimental.

Table 3.6: Interrelationship between squares

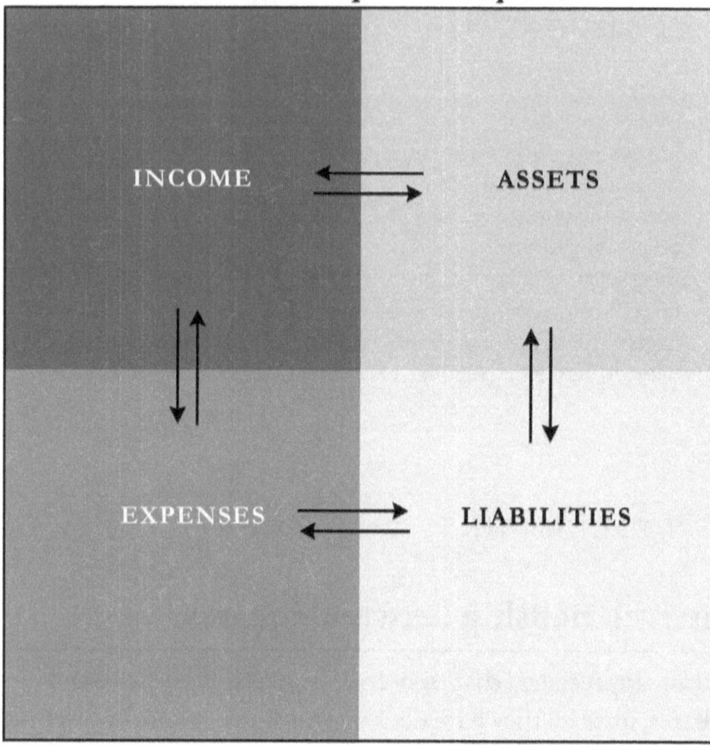

On the other hand, a liability like debt for real estate at low rates can give rise to an asset appreciating at an attractive rate.

Overall, by understanding these relationships, he can create a winning virtuous spiral.

Conclusion

Armed with the 4-square scorecard, Rahul has total financial information on one page and knows the current picture clearly and concisely. He realizes that it is a very useful first step, which will facilitate determining a winning strategy.

Part 2

Determining Strategy

Courtesy: The New Indian Express

How many runs will it produce today?

Chapter 4

Economic Cycle Staging - Assessing Pitch

Introduction

In his formative years, Rahul always found it interesting the way TV commentators (generally former players with considerable experience) sat down on the pitch and just before the start of a match, patted it lovingly and looked at the grass adoringly as if they were about to start grazing. Then they gazed into the camera and spoke interminably about cracks and crevices; essentially forecasting whether the pitch was good for batting and what the rival captains will do on winning the toss.

Now of course he realizes that assessing the pitch correctly is an important factor in determining an appropriate winning strategy. There are certain pitches where a very big total is possible, while others could be difficult necessitating a defensive approach. He will have to select his team and determine his batting order according to the nature of the pitch.

Just imagine a captain or a coach instructing their team to score at a brisk rate when the pitch is very difficult. They could lose wickets and get skittled out. It will be equally catastrophic if the pitch is good for making runs while the batsman is preserving his wicket and crawling along, again ensuring a heavy defeat.

Similarly, markets and economic conditions have phases which provide a good opportunity for making good returns and difficult phases during which wealth preservation is the more prudent course. Stocks and real estate, as we will see later in subsequent chapters, are top strikers, produce very good returns and in certain conducive phases of economic cycle should be deployed aggressively. On the other hand bonds, fixed income instruments and bank deposits are defensive instruments and produce small returns but in difficult phases of economic cycle should have a heavier part of the portfolio allocated to them. Sometimes the conditions will favour enhancement and sometimes just a preservation of what an individual has.

Consequently, one of the important strategic steps in the wealth game is assessing what stage of the economic cycle a country or the global economy is in.

February 20, 2004, Dambulla Stadium, Australia vs. Sri Lanka

Rahul was getting more and more surprised—he was following an intriguing match between Australia and Sri Lanka.

Australia, the world champions, known for their stroke-play were playing a very defensive game. Although they had lost only 1 wicket in the first 22 overs, they had scored only 114 runs. The trend continued and in 38 overs, despite losing only 2 wickets, their score was only 189. Rahul's intrigue deepened when he discovered that a fast scorer like Ricky Ponting scored only 58 runs in 82 balls although in terms of wickets they were in a very good position.

As he delved deeper, he discovered that the pitch was assisting spinners a lot, with a great deal of turn and bounce. Australia had read the pitch very well, assessed that a score of 225 would be a winning one. As a result, they eschewed their normal stroke-play, and conserved their wickets. By adopting this approach, they went on to score 262 for 6.

Had they gone in their usual way on this treacherous track they would have been all out for a meager total like 150.

Australia eventually won the match by getting Sri Lanka out for 178.

What is Economic Cycle?

Economic cycles consist of expansions occurring at about the same time in many economic activities, followed by similarly general contractions and then revivals that merge into the expansion stage of the next cycle. This sequence of changes is recurrent but not periodic. In duration economic cycles vary from more than one year to ten or twelve years.

Why Economic Cycles Always Exist

Economic cycles always exist. No expansion lasts for ever and similarly a contraction inevitably ends leading to an expansion. An expansion results from a simultaneous upswing in output, employment, sales and income. It is the co-movement of these variables that generates the cycle. For example, if income is up, consumers will spend more and corporate sales will increase. Companies will respond by revving up their output and also hiring more people. This will finally translate into more employment and better income thus leading to a virtuous spiral.

However, this virtuous spiral cannot continue forever. Overstretching of economic resources leading to undesirable outcomes like greater inflation eventually breaks it. The central bank starts putting brakes on the economy and the opposite cycle ensues. Consumers pull back on spending, businesses respond by producing less and cutting jobs, which lowers personal incomes, hurting consumer spending further, and reinforcing the downturn. Now it is a vicious spiral that again has to be broken by policy interventions.

Therefore the upswings and downturns of economic cycles are as certain as spring, summer, autumn, and winter; and continue in perpetuity.

Stages of an Economic Cycle

Some of the common stages of the economic cycle are:

- High growth, high employment, high sales, low inflation
- High growth, high employment, high sales, high inflation
- Low growth, low employment, low sales, high inflation
- Low growth, low employment, low sales, low inflation
- High growth, high employment, high sales, low inflation

There are various other permutations and combinations of all the factors mentioned above.

How to Know which Stage We are in?

We can assess the stage we are in by looking at the following economic factors:

- GDP growth rate
- Inflation rate
- Interest rates

- Currency strength
- Corporate earnings
- Stock market valuation

Why Economic Cycle Staging is Important for Investment Strategy?

Certain stages in an economic cycle are very conducive for earning high returns and not taking advantage of those opportunities will have a huge opportunity cost. After all, a target of 300 is not achieved by scoring an equal number of six runs in every over. On the other hand, it is achieved by a very judicious mix of attacking when the conditions are conducive and defending when a hostile bowler is at full throttle.

When economic conditions are good, top strikers like stocks and real estate have to be deployed, while defensive classes like debt or fixed income securities or bank deposits have to be given more prominence when tough economic conditions prevail.

When the economy is growing at a brisk rate, inflation is low and controlled, companies are doing well and their earnings are growing - this is a stage that is very good for stocks. On the other hand, an economy with a low growth rate and high inflation will be bad for stocks and there, a more defensive strategy of employing debt will be useful.

In-between stages are where a balanced allocation will be good.

Illustration of Indian Economy Staging - Jan. 2007

The Indian economy is presently growing at a very healthy rate of 8%. Inflation is fairly well controlled albeit picking up slightly. Interest rates are fairly stable and still on the lower side. RBI is fine-tuning its credit policy in relation to inflation expectations. The Indian Rupee is strong and stable. Corporates are doing well with a strong earnings growth momentum. Stock valuation ratios are still on the lower side (we will see these in detail in Chapter 8).

Overall a very clear verdict is that the present stage of the Indian economy is where lots of runs can be accumulated – stocks and real estate will do well. However, the conditions were very different just a few years back.

In year 2000, GDP growth rate was lower. Inflation was higher, accompanied by very high interest rates. The Indian Rupee was weakening and corporates were not so hot either. Stock valuations were on the higher side too. These conditions warranted a defensive approach with much more allocation to debt. Predictably, stocks took a major beating in the year 2000 and 2001 while debt instruments performed well in a falling interest rate environment.

Gradually the cycle started turning with GDP growth rate picking up and interest rates going much lower. Stocks have delivered remarkable returns in the last 4 years - 120% in the year 2003, relatively moderate 25% in 2004, picking up pace in 2005 with returns of 60% and 45% in 2006.

Conclusion

Rahul realizes that even before the play commences, an assessment of economic conditions is strategically important. It is useful since it essentially involves the ability to judge when to attack and when to defend.

What gives him added confidence is that only a broad and general assessment is very useful and he does not have to get into minute details. He just has to look at a few indicators, and those are available very easily.

He knows that this will be very useful for deploying different asset classes appropriately —another step forward in his quest for selecting and building a great team for victory.

Courtesy: Pradeep Mandhani/imageallsports.com

Courtesy: PTI

Different teams winning on different strengths: South Africa's Jonty Rhodes's superb fielding and Sri Lanka's Jayasuriya's fast scoring have steered their teams to victory many a time.

Chapter 5

Personal Life Cycle – Assessing Each Team's Strengths

Introduction

Rahul is aware that each team is different and can do well if it capitalizes on its strengths. For example, a team with rich batting resources can take a few more risks in run making than a team whose strength lies elsewhere. Other teams could have different strengths - the dominant West Indies team of 1980s had a battery of pace bowlers and they played with a full complement of 4 pace bowlers, never allowing the opposition batting to prosper. On the other hand, Australia, the current world champion team is full of stroke players who score runs fast and give their bowlers lots of time as well as runs for getting the opposition out. South Africa in their heyday capitalized on fantastic fielding led by Jonty Rhodes and could restrict run making by opposing teams.

Sri Lanka demonstrated the efficacy of capitalizing on individual strengths with their astonishing victory in the 1996 World Cup. Their main strength was explosive hitters combined with a lot of depth in batting. They decided that they could easily take the risk of scoring fast in initial overs. They sent in Jayasuriya and Kaluwitharana as openers with explicit instructions to hit out. Their strategy surprised quite a few teams as they marched to victory.

Similarly each person at any given moment of time is at his own individualized life stage. Life cycle factors including age, sex, marital status, number and age of children, occupation, hobbies, current income, net worth, values and aspirations determine what an individual's financial goals are. Additionally, desired lifestyle varies from one person to another. For one team, a total of 320 could be a losing proposition while for some, a total of 150 could be a winning one.

Financial strategy has to be fine-tuned and customized in order to be effective for different individuals. A young person can take more risks by allocating extensively to high yield but volatile instruments in the early part of his innings. He has lots of batting or earning opportunities left. However, a person about to retire has to look out for a monthly income and his risk-taking ability is much less. He necessarily has to invest in more stable, steady instruments. Dwelling on the importance of playing on one's strengths, Rahul's thoughts wander to...

March 2, 1996, Feroz Shah Kotla, Delhi, India vs. Sri Lanka

This was one of the league matches in the earlier stages of the World Cup. India was in good form and was expected to beat Sri Lanka comfortably. Sri Lanka won the toss and put India in to bat. India after a slow start and losing a wicket, performed very well. Sachin Tendulkar was in great form and went on to score a masterly 137 with a strike rate of 100. India finished with an imposing (considered a winning total in those days) of 271 for 3.

Here Sri Lanka sprang a surprise. They sent in Jayasuriya and Kaluwitharana who started hitting out ferociously right from the word go. Manoj Prabhakar got hit for 47 runs in 4 overs and was literally sent into retirement. In 15 overs Sri Lanka was 120 for 1. They started with a required run rate of 5.44 and had quickly brought it down to less than 4.5. In the end, captain Arjuna Ranatunga and Hashan Tilakratane easily took Sri Lanka to victory by 6 wickets in the 49th over. It is interesting to note that both these players batted at a comfortable rate. Ranatunga scored 46 runs in 63 balls while Tillakaratne scored 70 in 98. Their policy of taking measured risks in the early stages paid off, where they could preserve wealth at low risk in the latter part of the innings, thus emerging victorious.

Personal Life Cycle Staging

Personal life cycle can be staged in multiple ways. The three most common are:

Based on Age

A young 30-year-old, recently married, will like to have a stable income, normally secured by a job. He might also be thinking of having his own apartment. His interests might extend to a reserve fund for emergencies and a low cost life insurance. Ideally, he should also be accumulating assets and developing them for future needs. His risk taking capacity is high.

A person in his forties might be looking more actively for investments other than his personal residence. He will be concentrating on funds for his children's education. He will be more receptive to initiating a retirement program, focusing on growth and tax savings.

In his fifties, a person is about to retire and looks to establish a replacement for his monthly income. He is augmenting his retirement fund so that his retirement years are golden. He will be interested in completing payments on his home mortgage. He will concentrate his savings in instruments of moderate to low risk.

A person in his sixties might pare his basic lifestyle costs. He will concentrate on ensuring that he can pursue his retirement activities. His desire will be to remain active and retain his zest for life. He will settle his debts and manage his investment assets so as to keep pace with inflation. He will get his estate in order and simplify his financial affairs.

Based on Life Stage

Modigliani & Brumberg provided the following staging:

- Individual supported by parents
  - ☐ Income very low
  - ☐ Few financial decisions

    - For the parent to plan for some future needs and even more importantly to see some talent and nurture it
- Young Single
  - ☐ Income barely matches expenditures—no significant savings
  - ☐ Financial decisions tend to be mostly short term
  - ☐ Purchase car, clothes, music system
  - ☐ Budgeting is important
- Young Couple, No Children
  - ☐ Income greater than expenditures—some savings
  - ☐ Purchase home furnishings
  - ☐ Home purchase

- Couple With Children
  - ☐ Income approximately equal to expenditures
  - ☐ Upgrade house
  - ☐ Purchase children's toys, clothing, and supplies
  - ☐ Purchase life insurance
  - ☐ College tuition expenses
  - ☐ Debt management is important
- Empty Nesters
  - ☐ Income greater than expenditures
  - ☐ Purchase investments
  - ☐ Retirement planning is important
  - ☐ Tax considerations are important
- Retired
  - ☐ Income less than expenditures
  - ☐ Live off savings
  - ☐ Purchase medical and nursing services
  - ☐ Estate planning is important

Based on Wealth Stage

Accumulation stage

During this stage, individuals are looking to build wealth because their financial goals are quite far in the future and investments can be made for the long-term. Essentially, needs are distant and the primary aim is long-term wealth accumulation.

Middle stage

Here, while the individual is still accumulating wealth, one or more of his goals are fast approaching and clearly in sight, like child's education. This is the middle stage combining both accumulation and harvesting – quite a demanding stage.

Reaping stage

This is the cashing out stage, because the goal and purpose towards which the individual has invested have arrived. In essence, this is the time to reap the harvest he has sown. Retirement in many instances is the reaping stage where there is no further accumulation and lifestyle has to be supported by what has already been collected.

Importance of Personal Cycle Staging

Each individual is unique - he has a distinct set of circumstances, resources, attitudes, aspirations and needs. Therefore, only a customized strategy is effective. Life-cycle staging combined with wealth staging provides a clear picture of whether an individual at the present juncture is in a wealth creation or wealth preservation stage or a combination of two and in what proportion. This becomes a good early input for determining an effective winning strategy.

As we will see in subsequent chapters, different asset classes are appropriate and do well when matched with the right time horizon. For example, stocks deliver well if there is a reasonable time horizon and for real estate the time horizon is even longer. An appropriate matching of liabilities with the right asset classes is important. A good understanding of personal life-cycle stage provides a good estimate of time horizon for needs or liabilities.

Conclusion

Coming back to the present, Rahul realizes that to win he has to know his strengths and play to them. To be successful and emerge victorious, financial strategy has to be fine-tuned and customized in order to be effective for different individuals. Therefore, understanding the unique life and wealth staging of an individual is an important step. This will also facilitate determining specific financial goals, which is our next chapter.

Courtesy: Lester Anthony Paul

No target is insurmountable

Chapter 6

Identifying Financial Goals – Reaching Your Target

Introduction

Rahul, while preparing his team, also has to know his opposition thoroughly. What is the Financial Needs Team's strategy and how can he counter it? How should he define his goals and quantify them? He realizes that he has to set a target for his team and only then can they win. A well-defined target as compared to diffuse, ill defined one, helps focus the mind and ensure resources are employed optimally.

Researchers who have studied peak performance in individuals - executives, professionals, entrepreneurs, and sportspersons - have observed that the successful ones have one common characteristic: they set goals for themselves. Otherwise, one tends to live from day to day, muddling through or operating in mediocrity, with only the haziest notion of where one is going or what one really wants out of life.

Rahul is aware that quite a few matches have been lost because batsmen were not given any targets. Either they were too cautious even on an easy wicket, or they were too reckless. Similarly, the setting of financial goals is one of the most important aspects of winning the wealth game. Having well defined financial goals provides the necessary impetus for progress.

March 12, 2006, Johannesburg Park, Australia vs. South Africa

This is the most extraordinary and highest scoring one-dayer ever. Before this match, no team had scored more than 400 in ODIs.- Australia first created a world record by scoring 434 for 4. Incredibly, South Africa surpassed this difficult target by scoring 438 for 9. What made it even more exciting and nail biting was that it was the final match of the series that was tied at two games each.

Ponting won the toss and elected to bat. Gilchrist typically played a breezy knock of 55 runs in 44 balls and, in 15 overs they were 97 for 1. Ponting was scoring fast and had a good partnership with Katich; and in 30 overs, Australia was 216 for 2. Then an astonishing acceleration took place - Ponting and Hussey scored at the rate of 10 runs per over and took the score to 374 for 2. The last 4 overs produced a breathtaking 60 runs and Australia had a huge world record of 434 for 4. Ponting scored 164 in 105 balls and Hussey 81 in 51 balls.

South Africa had a big target but the pitch still remained a perfect batting strip. It was very conducive to blistering stroke play with a very fast outfield. The target was difficult but attainable. The mood in the dressing room was one of quiet determination. They had two main strikers in captain Graeme Smith and Herschelle Gibbs and both had to be utilized early in the innings. Also, there was no room for building up an innings - the run rate right from the word go had to be 9 runs per over or higher. They knew they had to go all out right from the start and fire on all cylinders. Not a single scoring opportunity could be missed.

They started poorly, losing Dippenaar in the second over.. That brought Smith and Gibbs together; and they took the score to 190 in 22 overs, thus maintaining the rate. Smith scored 90 in 55 balls. Gibbs along with De Villiers raised the tempo even further and in the next 8 overs scored 94 runs - almost 12 an over. Gibbs finally ended with 175 runs in only 111 balls. Now, with South Africa at 299 for 4 in 32 overs, there was no looking back. The match, of course, remained exciting till the end with the batting team losing wickets at regular intervals. They finally won with only one wicket and one ball to spare.

One of the biggest factors contributing to winning despite chasing a seemingly unattainable target was that there were no two ways. The target was huge and well defined and the path was only one. They had to hit out right from the beginning and there was no confusion, only a steely resolve. They had to be intensely focused and implement well.

Identifying Financial Goals

Rahul takes a visionary look at his finances and financial goals by thinking ahead for the next 20 years. What factors will help him regard himself as a winner? What achievements will he really treasure?

He engages in an inner dialogue about what is really important for him and his family. He wants financial security - a sense of not having to worry about meeting needs, being able to do what he wants when he wants. He desires a very good lifestyle even after retirement, akin to his current lifestyle. He wants to provide his children an excellent education to ensure an even better life for them. He wants a very comfortable home in a nice neighborhood. He wants to be able to take interesting vacations regularly.

He talks to many people with varying aspirations, backgrounds, and values. Their needs and wants might appear assorted and diverse, as hopping from one thing to another. However, unerringly in financial terms, three most important goals emerge:

- Maintaining a comfortable and independent retirement
- A nice home of their own in a location of their choice
- Providing quality education to their children and giving them a head start in life

Quantifying Financial Goals

Rahul now wants to put a figure to his targets. Working out how much money one will need to reach one's life goals will make them more real. He knows that he will be able to put in some concrete action steps only if he has an equally concrete target.

His vice captain is skeptical about the assumptions he will have to make regarding inflation, taxation and investment returns prevailing in the future, to be able to set his targets. Rahul tells him nonchalantly that it is important to think ahead even though it is not possible to predict a ball-by-ball scenario of any match. Real conditions may unfold differently, but pre-match strategizing has facilitated many victories, as any coach will vouch for.

Rahul takes the help of an example to understand how retirement requirements can be quantified. He is aware that different teams will require different amounts based on their income and resources. Somebody could be rating a comfortable retirement at Rs.30,000 and some at Rs.80,000 for their monthly expenditure. However, the approach for everybody will be similar. He goes through the following simple sequence:

a. *Visualizing Lifestyle Expenditures at Retirement*

The simplest way of estimating is to begin with the present pattern of expenditures and then to visualize in what respect the pattern will be different once one has retired.

For instance, health related expenses would be more. In other categories such as housing, clothing and food, expenses are likely to be lower. For example, housing loans might have been paid off completely or to a large extent and children related expenses are also likely to be minimal.

Table 6.1: Visualizing Retirement Expenses in Relation to Current Expenses

Monthly Expenses	Current	Retirement
Food	11000	9000
Clothing	7000	5000
Housing	10000	7000
Children related	11000	2000
Health & Insurance	5000	10000
Transportation	8000	6000
Appliances	8000	4000
Discretionary	10000	7000
Interest expense	5000	0
Total Expenses	75000	50000

In this illustration, retirement expenses are Rs. 50,000 per month.

b. *Years Left Before Retirement*

This is an easy step. A 40-year-old person in this example aiming to retire at the age 60years has 20 years left before retirement.

c. *Forecasting Inflation*

After 20 years, a lot more money will be required to buy what Rs. 50,000 buys today because of inflation. One useful way is to see the Indian Cost Inflation Indexation Table published annually by the Central Board of Direct Taxes, Department of Revenue, Government of India.

Table 6.2: *Cost Inflation Index*

FY	CII	FY	CII
1981–82	100	1994–95	259
1982–83	109	1995–96	281
1983–84	116	1996–97	305
1984–85	125	1997–98	331
1985–86	133	1998–99	351
1986–87	140	1999–00	389
1987–88	150	2000–01	406
1988–89	161	2001–02	426
1989–90	172	2002–03	447
1990–91	182	2003–04	463
1991–92	199	2004–05	480
1992–93	223	2005–06	497
1993–94	244		

Key:

FY = Financial Year

CII = Cost Inflation Index

Based on past trends and by assigning more weightage to the inflation index during the last three years, Rahul forecasts an average annualized inflation rate of 6 % for the next 20 years.

d. *Real Return and Power of Compounding*

Nominal return is the absolute return earned by an investment, while real return on an investment is the return above inflation. For example, an investment earning a nominal return of 6% with an inflation of 6% has a real return of absolutely 0. While an investment with a nominal rate of 15% and with same inflation rate of 6% will have a real return of 9 %.

To fund a retirement lifestyle 20 years later, which is similar to what Rs.50,000 will buy today in a month, with a real return of 0, exactly the same amount of money, namely Rs.50,000, will have to be set aside every month. On the other hand, with a nominal rate of 15% and a real return of 9%, the amount of monthly savings required to fund the same retirement lifestyle goes down drastically to less than 1/5th, namely Rs.9,750 every month. This goes down even further if saving for a long-term goal starts earlier.

Rahul is now more confident about winning this game. This very attainable real return target of 9% has lifted his spirits. He knows that he can maintain a good retirement lifestyle by saving an affordable sum every month. Moreover, it will not impinge on and affect his current lifestyle.

The same approach is applicable for analyzing all long-term goals. Housing has certain additional factors like buying for own usage or for investment. An additional issue is whether to buy or to rent. These issues are discussed in the chapter on Real Estate.

Essentially, it all comes down to generating a good real return since that drastically reduces the money required to be set aside for meeting future needs.

Conclusion

Rahul is glad that he has tried to size up the opposition. Now that he has identified his financial goals, he can marshal his resources appropriately.

Similarly, he knows that some of his assets have to be earmarked and invested appropriately to ensure a comfortable retirement lifestyle, desired housing, and excellent education for his children.

A very useful and comforting fact emerging from all this analysis is that Rahul's goals look a lot more attainable. They are no more daunting. Having defined the goals and the required real rate, the strategy to achieve them will be far more definite and consequently realizable. With newfound confidence, Rahul steps out of the realm of conjecture and hypothesis into the real world. He has assessed his opponent in depth and familiarized himself with its characteristics. Combined with knowledge of his own team's strengths and weaknesses, Rahul is well on the path to victory.

Courtesy: PTI

Celebrating success – the Indian Huddle, a psychological technique for enhancing team spirit and motivation

Chapter 7

Behavioural Finance - Cultivating a Winning Mindset

Introduction

August 10, 2005: The newspaper headlines screamed: 'New coach, new captain, yet the same old story'. India had lost yet another final from a winning position. By winning only one of the last 20 finals it played in, the Indian team was creating a dubious world record.

Rahul's desire to be a successful captain, repeatedly winning laurels, causes him to dwell on this very disturbing question — how many times have we seen India's cricket team get into winning positions only to be pipped at the post? It's time, perhaps, to probe whether these are but an unusually large number of unfortunate coincidences or whether it's symptomatic of something more sinister.

Words like 'Indians are good starters of the game but rarely show the ability to finish the game' from Murali, the great Sri Lankan bowler, make Rahul's ears burn. Most modern coaches, emphasize the mental aspect. They believe that this area can make a lot of difference in performance and thus, results.

Until recently, a typical cricketer knew that winning in cricket meant performing well in batting, bowling and fielding – he had never heard of psychology being used in cricket. However, times have changed. The Indian team in addition to a coach, enlisted the services of a couch man, Sandy Gordon. Sandy is a professor of psychology at the University of Western Australia and started advising the Indian team around the time of the World Cup. India had started very poorly in World Cup 2003. Their performance in the first two matches led to unprecedented crowd anger back home. Sandy's techniques including the team huddle contributed to the Indian team lifting itself and creditably reaching the final.

A typical investor similarly knew that successful wealth management involved a good knowledge of economics, accounting, and mathematics. He had never visualized that psychological factors might be affecting his investment returns.

Ever since the 1992 reforms, the Indian pitch has been remarkable. For example, good Indian mutual funds investing in stocks have provided compounded annualized returns of 27% for the last 13 years — among the best returns worldwide and that too, sustained over such a long time. However, the Indian investor has utilized this pitch rather poorly. He has repeatedly failed to convert good starts into anything meaningful - he has exited early. Many times, he has refused to even participate by assuming that the pitch is very hostile. Frequently, he has been unduly cautious. On the whole, very few investors have benefited from this remarkable scenario. On the other hand, many of them have been on the losing side.

What explains this anomaly? The finance profession is increasingly aware that psychological factors can thwart rational analysis and prevent investors from achieving the best results for their portfolio. Every investment is an emotional as well as a financial commitment. Study of these psychological factors is the new field of 'Behavioral Finance'.

August 9, 2005, Premdasa Stadium, Colombo, India vs. Sri Lanka

Sri Lanka started batting on a good pitch but lost Attapattu early. There was a very good knock from swashbuckling Jayasuriya, who also completed 10,000 runs in one-day internationals during this knock - only the 4th man to do so. Subsequently, Jayawardene and Arnold had a 125 run fifth wicket partnership, enabling Sri Lanka to score 281 for 9 in 50 overs.

India began very well with Sehwag scoring 48 runs in 22 balls and reducing the required run rate to a very manageable one. Good contributions from Rahul Dravid and Yuvraj Singh took the score to 186 for 2. With 8 wickets in hand and an average required run rate of 4.8, India was finally all set to win a final. But what really happened? Dravid's departure exposed the middle order that panicked and collapsed under pressure. India finally ended at 263 for 9, losing the match by 18 runs. Thus caving in to pressure and losing yet another final. Not being able to keep their mental composure was one of the important contributory factors.

Behavioural Finance

This is the field that studies how people's mental attitudes affect how they earn, save and invest money. Traditionally, economic theory is built on the premise that everybody acts in a totally rational manner.

In the late 1970s, two psychologists, Amos Tversky and Daniel Kahneman, noted that many individuals did not behave as traditional economic theory predicted. They developed a new model of how individuals actually behave and make decisions when faced with uncertainty. They named their model 'Prospect theory'. Emotions of fear, greed, uncertainty, loss aversion frequently cloud the rational decision making process.

Figure 7.1: The Emotions of Investing

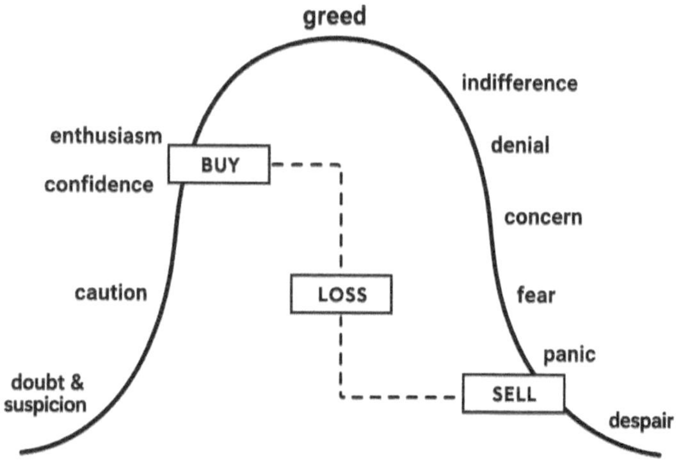

Behavioral finance has assumed great importance lately; and the 2002 Nobel Prize for Economics went to Daniel Kahneman for his work in this field. This field essentially tries to identify and study behavioral traps and patterns in irrational economic decisions and to determine what can be done to minimize the intrusion of such traps.

Common Behavioural Traps

Herding Instinct

Herding instinct is the tendency of individuals to adapt their thinking to the prevailing opinion. It is very hard to remain distinct from the crowd. This stems from disbelief that a large group of people could be wrong, a belief that someone knows something, and a conviction that they should not miss out on it.

Others influence an investor's decision. Therefore, fads and fashions have a great impact on investor decisions. Investors tend to buy or sell when they see or perceive lots of people doing the same. Consequently, mood or market sentiment becomes an important factor. It also causes excess fluctuations or volatility, which cannot be explained by fluctuations in economic factors such as dividends or earnings. Market sentiment causes the markets to overshoot in either direction.

Extreme examples of herding instinct have led to major stock bubbles in the past. These include Tulip mania in Holland, South Sea bubble in England, and very recently, the worldwide Internet bubble of 1999-2000.

Self-Attribution Bias

If a decision has gone right, most investors believe that it was their own acumen, which resulted in such a decision. They might give very little credit to favorable environmental factors prevailing at that time. Investors with a high degree of self-attribution bias, find it very difficult to bail out at the right time. Therefore, they rise with the market and fall with the market.

For example, in the technology bubble of 1999, quite a few investors believed that they were making all the right calls. Even a high profile Indian fund manager in a speech in Toronto in March 2000 was extolling his stock-picking abilities, without realizing that in a few days' time, his technology fund would show rapid erosion.

Representative bias

Too many parallels could be erroneously drawn between events that seem the same, but are actually very different. For example, many investors believed that Sensex at 6000 in the year 2004 was similar to Sensex reaching 6000 in the year 2000. In reality, the two situations could not have been more different. Sensex was highly overvalued in year 2000 with a P/E ratio of 29, while being undervalued in the year 2004. Many investors balked at this entry level and missed out on a hugely profitable trade.

Cognitive Dissonance

This is the discomfort that investors encounter when they confront evidence that conflicts with their view. The natural tendency is to minimize this discomfort and results in a propensity to shut out bad news. For example, an investor having a position in a particular stock or market might be in denial mode regarding any bad news concerning his holdings. It might be too late by the time he comes out of his state of denial.

Loss Aversion

Investors generally have a aversion to realizing a loss. They tend to hold on to a position in the hope that it will turn around one day. Therefore, investors run their losses while taking profits quickly. Research confirms this fact of investors selling their stocks for a gain much more frequently than they do for a loss.

Anchoring

When an investor buys a stock, he opens a mental account with the purchase price as the reference point. He anchors himself to a price and his future decisions may be based on this anchor. If the price goes below the anchor, he can be easily persuaded to buy more to improve his average.

How can the Investor Overcome Behavioural Traps?

Investors can study their behavior patterns to see whether they are falling into these traps and therefore, taking poor decisions. The following rules can help:

Decisions on a forward-looking basis

Rather than looking at the past trades, decisions should be on a forward-looking basis. What are the future prospects of an investment? Mental accounting, anchoring, or reference to the purchase price should not be considerations for decision-making.

Long-term orientation

Many attractive asset classes like stocks and real estate are much more predictable in the long term, while being unpredictable in the short term. There is a lot more uncertainty in the short term. Generally, investors fall into behavioral traps when faced with decision-making under uncertainty. A long-term orientation as compared to overtrading is very effective in garnering the immense potential of various asset classes.

Not to follow the herd blindly

There have been so many instances when the herd has been wrong. Basing decisions on fundamental factors as compared to following the herd blindly is beneficial. For example, everybody wanted to participate in the overvalued markets of the year 2000. Contrastingly, nobody wanted to enjoy the huge rally of the Sensex at a grossly undervalued 2800. The same investors were all desperate to get in at levels of 14000.

Precommitment & Discipline

Investors should set up rules and incentives to keep investments on track. For example, an investor might decide to place 10% of his savings in liquid instruments for emergency needs. He also might decide to put 25% in very safe instruments. The rest he wants to utilize for generating good returns. Also, there, he might allocate 40% to stocks and the rest to other classes like real estate and commodities. It will be important to adhere to these pre-committed allocations. If stocks go up faster than other instruments, their weightage in the portfolio will increase. It is important for the investor to be disciplined and bring the levels back to his pre-committed levels. He should not alter his allocation out of emotion; it should be tinkered with only if market factors have altered in a fundamental way.

Conclusion

The individual investor falls into psychological traps that prevent him from being an effective investor. Rahul's awareness of his attitudes toward money can go a long way toward better portfolio performance. On one hand, his anxiety about investing is much less; on the other, he is looking forward to playing an enjoyable and profitable game.

This healthy attitude towards money and the winning mindset will facilitate a very effective selection of the team - that is our next important section.

Part 3

Selecting the Team

Courtesy: The New Indian Express

Sachin Tendulkar - The Top Striker

Chapter 8

Stocks – The Top Strikers

Rahul is intrigued by players like Tendulkar, Gilchrist, Ponting, Gibbs and Lara, who manage to score fast and at the same time, are prolific run makers. How is it possible to score consistently and that too, at a fast pace? Is it not contrary to the common wisdom that by playing cautiously, you will be able to accumulate more runs?

Looking at statistics, we see that the top batsmen have good strike rates (runs scored per 100 balls) along with equally good averages (runs scored per innings). This proves that a skilled batsman scores more runs and that, too, at a faster rate. In financial terms, he is demonstrating that it is possible to produce great returns at minimal risk.

Table 8.1: Consistency Combined with Fast Scoring

Player	Average runs per innings	Strike rate-runs per 100 balls
Brian Lara	42.63	79.81
Sanath Jayasuria	31.92	88.71
Sachin Tendulkar	44.84	85.83
Adam Gilchrist	35.71	94.66
Ricky Ponting	41.28	77.32
Sourav Ganguly	41.83	74.38
Virendra Sehwag	32.28	94.88
Inzamam-ul-Haq	39.65	73.62

Akin to these dashing yet reliable batsmen, stocks are the most effective wealth creators piling up good returns with minimal risk. Historical returns over long periods of time and in different countries including India, show stocks producing maximum risk adjusted returns compared to any other asset class.

Therefore, stocks have to be an integral part of every portfolio. Just imagine Australia playing without Gilchrist and Ponting, India playing without Tendulkar in his prime or West Indies playing without Lara when at his best. Stocks occupy the same crucial role in a winning portfolio

However, there is a batting technique that sets these batsmen apart. When a batsman walks in, his single objective is to put on as many runs as possible. But at the same time, there are risks. He has to choose the right balls to hit and select the right shots. He also has to adapt to pitch conditions. If he goes for runs indiscriminately, he can lose his wicket.

Similarly, stocks have their pitfalls. They do not move in a straight line, but go up and down. Their volatile nature produces a few jitters for the investors and there is ample scope for making mistakes.

But just by following some easy principles of stock investing, the immense potential of stocks can be harnessed at minimal risk.

The ability to deploy them effectively can easily be the difference between winning and losing. Learning this will be Rahul's major focus in this chapter.

March 1, 2003, Centurion Park, South Africa India vs. Pakistan, World Cup Quarterfinal

Pakistan wins the toss and elects to bat under good conditions. Around Saeed Anwar's century, they build up a good total of 273 for 7 in their 50 overs. In a way India now has to support an extravagant lifestyle as they were quite generous in the field. They have to score whenever the conditions are conducive for run making.

Stocks (top strikers) have to be deployed effectively, especially in the first 15 overs. Just to recapitulate, the fielding side has major restrictions in the first 15 overs and there is scope to hit lots of boundaries. Therefore, the allocation plan is to send the two best strikers, Sehwag and Tendulkar to open the innings when the valuation is favoring them.

India gets off to a good start with 50 being scored in the first five overs. Sehwag and Ganguly get out soon after and some stability is required. Kaif, a defensive player akin to a bond, is sent. Tendulkar is hitting at a good pace while Kaif is blocking. They have a 102-run stand and take the score to 155 in 21 overs.

In the remaining 29 overs, only 119 runs are required to win, implying a modest run rate of little more than 4. Therefore, risks can be eschewed and the match can still be won. Dravid plays intelligently, scores at a steady pace without taking much risk, and along with Yuvraj, takes India to victory in the 46th over.

This demonstrates a very carefully planned approach. During the first 15 overs when run-making opportunities were immense, top strikers were deployed. This is similar to when the stock market is attractive on the valuation front and aggressive allocation to stocks is warranted. This can be compared to the situation in 2003 when economic conditions favoured stocks tremendously. Stocks were undervalued while bonds were overpriced. Stocks delivered 120% that year.

The good start was leveraged in a very well thought out manner. It brought down the required run rate considerably. Steady instruments like Dravid and Kaif were deployed subsequently to win the match comfortably. An investor, who gained from an upsurge in stocks and is close to attaining his financial goals, should then transfer some of his assets from stocks to bonds. In this way, he realizes profits on stocks, reduces his portfolio risk, and increases the probability of attaining his financial goals.

What are Stocks?

Stock is one of the two major sources of financing for a company, the other being debt. The difference between the two is that through stocks one buys ownership in a company, whereas in case of debt, the investor is lending money to the company. Equity is also a term used for stocks, especially in USA, signifying that stockholders hold proportionate equitable rights

When the firm borrows, it promises to repay the debt with interest. If it doesn't keep its promise, the debt holders may force the firm into bankruptcy. However, no such commitments are made to the stockholders. They are entitled to whatever is left over after the debt holders have been paid off.

Sale of new stock by the firm occurs in the primary market. Large companies usually arrange for their stocks to be listed on stock exchanges. Stock exchanges are the secondary markets that allow investors to trade existing stocks amongst themselves.

Stock index is a representative number that indicates changes in the stock market over a period of time. A broad index can represent the whole economy and sectoral indices could represent different sectors of the economy. Another index can depict any particular group based on a specific criterion; for example, a mid cap index comprises stocks which are in a certain range of market capitalization (for example, it could be Rs. 200 crores to 1000 crores for a mid cap index).

The popular Sensex and Nifty are diversified indices representing the broad Indian market. For them to accurately reflect the broad market, they have to include a sufficient number of companies so that the impact of any single company is minimal. Additionally, their composition has to be close to real proportional representation of different economic sectors.

Stock Return and Risk

Stock Return

For the stockholders, the source of future cash flows is the profits of firms. They do well if the company generates good profits and they participate proportionately in a company's progress.

Profits create value for shareholders mainly by:

- Payment of cash dividends
- Price of the share going up on expectation of good future performance and a healthy earnings growth, thus giving rise to capital gains

Example

Suppose if an investor has paid Rs. 10 to buy 1 share of a company and after one year the company gives him a dividend of Rs. 0.5. Additionally, the stock price goes up to Rs. 11. Effective rate of return is 15%, with 10% coming from the capital gains and 5% from the dividends.

Stock Risk

It is mainly the price risk, since stock prices are very volatile. This price risk can be divided into:

- Company-specific - Something goes wrong with the company in whose stock the investor has invested. It can lose market share, a strong competitor gets in, a new disruptive technology is introduced, it loses a key person and many other causes.
- Sector specific - Some negative development affecting a whole sector takes place. For example, patent law changes can affect the whole pharmaceutical sector. Development of alternative energy sources can have a major bearing on the oil and petroleum sector.
- Market level risk - This is a risk relating to adverse developments in a country. For example, political instability will affect the whole market. Similarly, faulty macroeconomic policies or a recession can bring every sector down.

Recognizing these risks separately is important, since diversifying by investing in several stocks belonging to multiple sectors reduces the company and sector specific risks. A diversified portfolio will be subject mainly to market level risk.

Stock Valuation - P/E Ratio

Valuation of stocks is not precise and that is because of market sentiment. Like everything else that is traded actively, demand-supply factors play an important role. Multiple participants with their different motivations look at the market in their own different ways. This is what contributes to what is commonly referred to as 'market sentiment'.

The stock price is based on the company's performance incorporating various dimensions and growth prospects going forward. An estimation of higher future profits will put a greater value on the company's stock. Valuation measures commonly employed by market participants give the price a mooring. The market has a tendency to move towards its fundamental value. The further away it is, in either direction, the stronger will be the pull for it to come back.

Price-Earnings ratio (P/E ratio) is the most basic and fundamental yardstick for valuing stocks. It is simply the ratio of the price of a share to the annual earnings per share. For example, you buy a company's share for Rs. 100. This company's earnings per share is 8. Therefore, P/E ratio of this company will be 12.5. In other words, you are paying Rs. 100 to earn Rs. 8. Therefore, earnings yield, which is inverse of price-earnings ratio, is 8%. A P/E ratio of 20 implies a yield of 5%. P/E ratio is a very useful predictor of future returns in the long run.

Dynamism and fluidity of a stock price result from earnings not being static. Estimate of future expected earnings plays an important role. If economic conditions of a country improve, if a particular industry suddenly takes off or a company comes with a blockbuster new product, the future earnings will be much higher. If the company is now expected to make Rs. 15/share next year, the share price might zoom to Rs. 150 with better sentiment moving the P/E ratio also to a higher level of 10.

While P/E ratio is very useful as a valuation parameter, it has to be looked at in conjunction with other factors. A low P/E might not be indicating lots of hidden value; it might be showing a poorly performing company. Similarly, a high P/E might not always mean overvaluation; it might indicate expectation of a faster earnings growth. Peer comparisons of this ratio are very useful, especially with companies with similar profiles and in the same industry. Any P/E valuation sticking out like a sore thumb should be the starting point for a detailed analysis of factors causing such a deviation.

A very useful ratio is PEG that is calculated by dividing P/E ratio by the earnings growth rate. If P/E ratio of a company is 15 and its earnings are growing at 20%, then one might have found a bargain. A lower PEG will be attractive, preferably 0.5 or less, but certainly less than 1. Some high growth companies get quoted at astronomical P/E ratios of 60-70. Stock prices of such companies will be very vulnerable since a company will find such a growth rate unsustainable over the long term, especially as it grows bigger in size. That gives rise to GARP (growth at reasonable price) concept that growth is important but it stock should be bought only at a reasonable price.

Consistent Stock Performance Worldwide

Looking at USA is instructive because of the very long history available. Jeremy Siegel in his widely acclaimed and intensely researched book 'Stocks for the Long Run' analyzed the total return indexes for stocks, long-term and short-term bonds, gold and commodities from 1802 through 2001. His research conclusively demonstrates that the total return on stocks overwhelmingly

Figure 8.1: Total Nominal Return Indices, 1801-2001

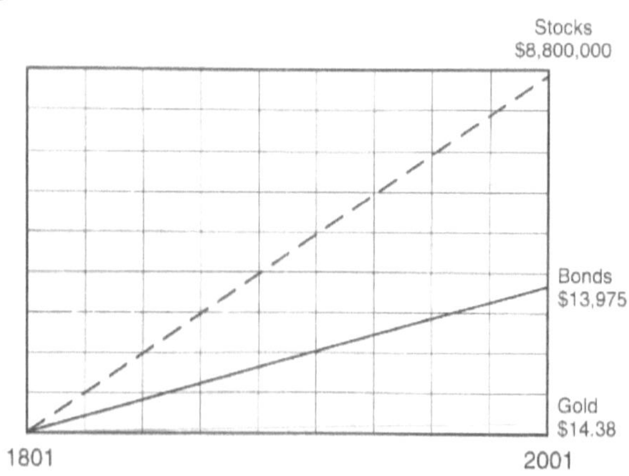

Source: 'Stocks for the Long Run' by Jeremy Siegel

dominates all other assets. One dollar invested and reinvested in stocks since 1802 would be nearly 8.8 million dollars by the end of 2001. Contrastingly, the same money invested in bonds would have given only 13975 dollars; in gold it would have been worth 14.38 dollars.

Stocks have been observed to perform similarly in other countries. Even the stock returns of Germany and Japan, devastated by World War II, bounced back to challenge the total return of stocks in the United States and the United Kingdom since the 1920s.

In addition to global dominance of stocks over other assets, the stock returns show remarkable long-term stability. Despite extraordinary changes in the economic, social, and political environments over the last two centuries, stocks have yielded around 7 % real (after inflation) annual returns.

The reason for the consistency of stock returns over time and countries is explained by an economic system, which is dependent on good corporate performance. Only those companies survive that have the ability to post a profitable performance in a rapidly changing environment. It is logical to assume that as economic output (measured by GDP (Gross Domestic Product)) rises, market valuations of corporations contributing to this growth should also rise.

The India story of stock returns is very similar. After gaining independence in 1947 and till the fifth plan (1974-79), the economy showed an annual growth of about 3%. It shifted into a higher gear in the late seventies, to a rate of 4.5–5%. The real boost came with drastic reforms initiated in 1992. In 2005, the economy grew at about 8% and expectations are for even faster growth in 2007.

India's first major stock index, Sensex, whose benign full form is 'Sensitive Index', was launched on January 2, 1986. It comprised 30 highly liquid stocks. On July 25, 1990, it touched the 1000 mark for the first time. In 16 years, it has gone up more than 12 times. Typically, growth has been spiky and uneven. On January

15, 1992, it crossed the 2000 mark following the liberal economic reforms announced by the government. Crossing 4000 took only two and a half months more. Then in the aftermath of Indian stock scam of 1992, it corrected and consolidated. However, in Y2K and with the Internet euphoria, it touched a high of 6200 only to fall to 2800. From late 2002, it has steadily gone up to reach a level of 8800 in October 2005 and to 12600 in May 2006. During the same month, a sharp, swift and deep correction brought it down to below 9000 before it staged a partial recovery. However, it recovered well to a level of 13725 in November 2006.

Overall, consistent with the stock performance almost everywhere, Indian stocks have delivered impressive performance over a long period of time. They could also be easily characterized as top strikers. As we will see later in the chapter, Indian stock mutual funds have done even better by outperforming indices.

Three Principles of Investing in Stocks

1 Valuation

The first principle is valuation of the stock market. Like for anything else, the first step is to evaluate whether the thing you intend buying is undervalued or overvalued.

An effective and fast way is to look at valuation ratios of important stock indices like Sensex and Nifty. It is not the index value which determines the valuation, but the ratios of P/E and PEG described earlier in the chapter that are useful. Movements of Sensex during the last 6 years illustrate this principle nicely.

Sensex's weighted average P/E has a historical range of 11-28. In Feb. 2000 at the time of the worldwide Internet bubble, all the valuation ratios were close to their historical tops. Quite a few analysts had started calling the market overvalued and the stock market had a precipitous fall.

Contrastingly, almost four years later, when Sensex was again trading at around 6300, similar to the levels of year 2000, P/E ratios were much lower. Also, PEG was very attractive. Therefore, the verdict was that the market was undervalued. Even in Sep. 2005, with a much higher level of 8700-8800, P/E ratio was only 17. It was much lower than the P/E level of 28 with a Sensex level of 6200 in Feb. 2000. In the last 5 years, Indian corporate earnings have surged, thus bringing down valuation ratios even at higher Sensex level.

Table 8.2: Valuation Example

Date	Sensex	P/E	PEG	Verdict	Subsequent Move
Feb. 2000	6200	28	1.9	overvalued	Big downward move for 3 years
Dec. 2002	3400	14.37	0.5	undervalued	125% returns in year 2003
Aug. 2004	5200	15.38	0.62	undervalued	moved up significantly
Dec. 2005	8200	16.43	0.65	undervalued	moved up significantly
May 2006	12610	22.1	0.95	in balance	corrected sharply
July 2006	10900	19.8	0.88	in balance	trend still up
Nov. 2006	13600	22.2	0.95	in balance	trend still up but selective and with corrections

Source: Finance Doctor

In May 2006, Sensex surged to a level around 12600 with a P/E ratio of almost 22. Earnings growth still had a momentum of 25%. With interest rates going up globally including India, earnings growth momentum could have slowed. With a PEG ratio threatening to cross the important level of 1, intense profit taking and a consequent sharp correction ensued. However, good economic fundamentals reasserted and Sensex recovered quickly.

2 Time-Horizon

The second important principle is that the time horizon for investing in stocks should be a long one. This is because of three important characteristics:

- Stocks are volatile. They do not move in a straight line. They go up and then come down, they can consolidate in a range for quite some time; and their short-term movements can be quite unpredictable.

Figure 8.2: Movement of Stocks

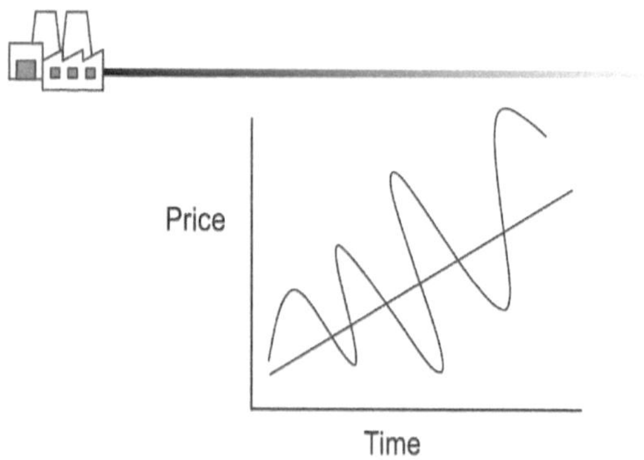

Source: Finance Doctor

Note: There is a smooth upward slope for stocks in the long run while at the same time there is lots of volatility in the short-term.

- Historically, over long periods of time and in multiple different markets, stocks have generated consistent and significantly positive returns. Their price movement depiction in a schematic manner is shown in Figure 8.2.

- Stocks also move in a spiky fashion. Peter Lynch in his best-selling book 'One up on Wall Street' states- "If an investor had invested $100,000 in the USA stock index on July 1, 1994 for five years, his money would have grown to $ 341,722. But if he was out of stocks for just 30 days over that stretch—those 30 days when stocks had their biggest gains—his money would have grown to only $153,792". Similarly in the Indian market, year 2003 was one of significant gains, much more than the subsequent years. Within 2003 too, there were big variations with a couple of big months.

Table 8.3: Stock Returns & Market Timing
Worst possible time to invest in stocks—22nd February, 2000—NAV Rs. 30.78
• 17th September, 2001—NAV Rs.15.02 • 10th June, 2005—NAV Rs. 64.23 • 14th October, 2005—NAV Rs. 79.3 • April 26, 2006—NAV Rs. 117.25 • July 5, 2006—NAV Rs. 102.57 • Nov. 21, 2006—NAV Rs. 127.77

Source: Finance Doctor

Note: Investors who bought this Indian fund In February 2000, at the peak of a cycle and the worst possible time for investing in stocks, at Rs.30.78, lost more than half of their investment- it was down to Rs.15.02 by Sept. 2001. The same fund in Nov. 2006 was more than 8 times at Rs.127.77. Obviously, the next wave has taken the value way past the previous high.

The combination of volatility in the short term, predictability of returns in the long run and not knowing when the big move would occur makes a longer investment horizon for stocks much more useful.

3 Diversification

Putting all your eggs in one basket is not advisable. Harry Markowitz won the Nobel Prize for his diversification theory in 1991. Simply put, the risk of a portfolio declines if two assets are combined that do not move in tandem and have a low correlation with each other.

For example, an investor believes that Ranbaxy Pharmaceuticals will provide good returns and invests his entire stock allocation amount in one stock. By doing so, he has assumed a huge company specific risk. His portfolio is very vulnerable to anything going wrong with that one company.

When apprised of this, he also invests in Dr. Reddy's Laboratories. Now his dependence on one company is less. However, he has a huge sector-specific risk. If the government announces that all medicine prices have been frozen, both his companies will be affected and the portfolio will take a major hit.

Instead, if he has a market portfolio comprising 15-20 stocks of various sectors, then he has diversified the company specific risk and sector specific risk; and is left only with market risk, which is the risk of broad economy.

Implementation - When to Enter and When to Exit

Entering the Market–Systematic and Lump-Sum Investing

There are two kinds of cash flows which can be invested:

- Periodic cash flows like savings from monthly income
- Lump sum

Systematic Investment Plan (SIP)

Assume that Rs.5000 is available every month as savings. Here there is a clear advantage in not trying to time the market and instead investing every month.

The stock market, as we have seen, has an upward trajectory. However, it has a tortuous and volatile climb, which is rather unpredictable in the short-term. Therefore, the averaging effect of investing at regular intervals is very useful. For example, in June 2006, the market was trading around 10000 levels. We rate our pitch conditions to be still favorable and therefore expect the index to go to higher levels over the next two years. However, there are some risk factors like higher interest rates and global oil prices. So the future path is unpredictable and not known. It is possible that the index goes down to 9000 and then goes up. On the other hand, it can go up directly and quickly.

To elaborate, while the destination is pretty certain, the path or timing is not. Systematic investing averages out the level at which funds have been invested. Besides, the investor is not wasting time and effort in trying to forecast or time his entry in the market. It also induces saving discipline by ensuring that a sum is set aside as savings every month. Besides, over a period of time, periodic savings can generate a significant amount. For example, if Rs. 5000 per month was invested for 150 months from Dec. 1993, to May 2006, in Franklin Prima Fund, one of the good diversified Indian mid cap stock funds, it would have grown to a sum of Rs. 70.55 lakhs, implying a compounded annualized return of 32.5%.

Lump Sum Investment

Suppose an investor has a lump sum to invest. Let's assume that economic conditions, personal conditions and time horizon all favor stock allocation. In such a scenario, attempting to time the market is futile and difficult, since there is 50% probability that the market will move up from here and 50% that it will go down before resuming its ascent. Investor should just go ahead as long as he is observing all three principles of investing in stocks.

The important thing is that if the fundamentals and valuation ratios are favourable, then it is better to invest when cash flow is available rather than fretting about entry levels. These decisions balance out in the long run. In half of these decisions, one would have missed out on the opportunity to invest at current levels, and in half, one could have invested at a lower value.

Exiting the Market - Preserving Profits

This is a major question, which confuses and mystifies many participants in the stock market. They rightly feel that it is impossible to determine the lowest or highest points of any cyclical move in the stock market. There is great subjectivity in the markets. Analysts spending all their time in forecasting and allocating tremendous resources are not much wiser. However, the good news is within this complexity, lay the roots of a simple solution for the investor. Spending lots of time and thought on determining precise entry and profit taking levels is futile. On the other hand, some simple monitoring will take care of a major part of the objectives.

The investor should just keep an eye on the valuation ratios for the index as well as individual stocks in his portfolio. There also, if only one ratio has to be looked at, it should be the P/E ratio. Further, if investment is through diversified mutual funds, then one needs to look at valuation ratios for the broad market only, rather than multiple stocks. The index can be monitored very easily while spending minimal time.

Index valuation ratios are reported every day in the financial newspapers and take only a couple of minutes to look up. This information provides a very good handle on what is going on, the right questions to ask, and in determining the current stage of the economic cycle. These couple of minutes looking at basic ratios have a disproportionately high utility for the investor.

Figure 8.3: When to Exit-Preserving Profits

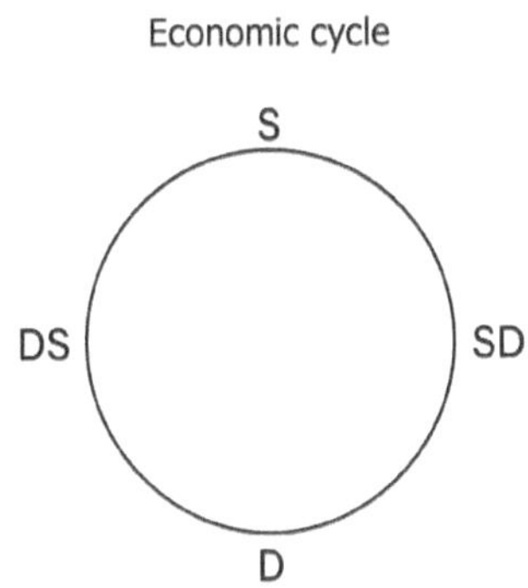

Source: Finance Doctor

The above allocation tool shows S point that is heavy stock allocation point with the market P/E ratio at the lower end of the range. D point denotes a very heavy allocation to Debt. As the economic cycle progresses, P/E ratio increases and that warrants moving part of the portfolio from stocks to debt. SD and DS points are almost equal allocations to stock and debt. S point can be compared with 2003 when Sensex was at 3000 with very low P/E ratio. D point was in Feb. 2000, when P/E ratio was at 28 and Bond yields were at 14%.

As the price/earnings ratio moves up, the allocation to stocks should steadily decrease. This will automatically entail profit taking. This helps investors preservation of profits, which is one of the most important tenets— there is no point going up with the market and coming down with the market.

Also, profit preservation should be linked to personal financial goals. This is best illustrated by an example—suppose an investor is investing money for his child's education. The money is required in the year 2010. He started investing in 2003 when Sensex was at 4300 and had a heavy allocation in stocks because the stock market was undervalued. Because of the good run in stocks, he is now very close to achieving his goal and winning the match. He should then pace his innings accordingly. To reach his objective, even a lesser allocation in stocks is sufficient. It is only prudent that he should preserve part of his profits by shifting a percentage of his portfolio to fixed income securities and preserve his profits, even if the long-term trend for stocks is still considered to be up.

Equity Funds - Mutual Funds Investing In Stocks

Investor has two alternatives to express his interest in stocks, either through stocks directly or through Equity Funds. It is his personal choice as long as he observing all three principles of investing in stocks.

Companies have to be analyzed in detail. The nature of their business, the economic sector they operate in, their position within the industry, sales and earnings growth, quality of management, strategic objectives, government regulation affecting their businesses, all have to be studied. Valuation measures like P/E ratios, PEG, and other measures have to be analyzed.

In direct investing, he retains control over choice of stocks and when to buy and sell. However, diversification by investing in at least 15-20 stocks belonging to various sectors is necessary for reducing the risk. Researching such a number of stocks can be very time-consuming.

Table 8.4: History of an Indian Stock Fund

Date	N A V	Market view
Dec. '93	4.69	Introduction of Fund
Apr. '95	10.10	Reforms progressing well
Feb. '97	5.00	*Slow* implementation of reforms
Feb. '00	30.78	Indian technology, internet, new millennium
Sep. '01	15.02	Global melt down
Dec. '02	23.31	Early signs of Indian corporate resurgence
Dec. '03	51.42	Second stage of reforms, good earnings growth
Apr. 23. '04	56.75	India shining, NDA expected to win
May 17, '04	43.51	Surprising election results
Oct. 4, '04	54.98	Reforms seen as irreversible
Oct. 14, '05	79.43	Economy growing at 8%, corporate earnings surging
Nov. 21, '06	127.77	Fundamentals still good, valuation ratios slightly higher

Source: Finance Doctor

Note: This fund has provided a tremendous return of 29.12% compounded annually since its inception in December 1993. This is one of the best performances globally, with Rs. 10 lakhs kept in the fund at that time amounting to Rs. 2.72 crores in Nov. 2006 (more than 27 times in less than 13 years).

Alternatively, he might prefer to outsource this research to mutual funds. In India, active funds have outperformed the index significantly and it is instructive to look at the performance of a major diversified Indian equity fund, as shown in the Table 8.4.

Equity funds can be classified along two dimensions:

- **Size of the stock:** Stocks could be large, mid-sized or small as measured by their market capitalization. Market capitalization is the number of shares multiplied by the stock price.
- **Investment Style:** This can be focusing on value, growth or a combination of the two.

Stocks that exhibit low P/E ratios are often called value stocks, whereas those with high P/E ratios are called growth stocks. These designations are not dependent on the products the firms make. Therefore, a technology stock although belonging to a high growth industry, could be classified as value stock, if it is selling at a low P/E ratio. Same stock could go through value and growth designations as its price fluctuates.

Funds will be combinations of these two main dimensions. Some of the common categories of Indian funds are:

Diversified Equity Funds

This is a category which is most common. It has the mandate to invest across all sectors of economy. This category has done very well with impressive returns. As a category, 5-year returns have been around 41% on a compounded annual basis. Diversified funds could further be divided into large cap, mid cap, and small cap funds. As the names suggest, these invest in large, mid, and small stocks respectively.

Some examples of excellent large cap funds with consistent performance over a number of years are Franklin India Bluechip, HDFC Equity, and Reliance Vision. Their returns range around 50%. Excellent mid cap funds with a long history include Franklin Prima and Reliance Growth. These funds have astounding 5-year returns of more than 60%. Sundaram Select Midcap has performed well since its initiation in 2002.

All returns are stated in compounded annualized terms.

Index Funds

They invest in stocks which are part of an index and mirror the index as precisely as possible. Their management fees are much less since there is no active management. Their average returns naturally have tracked the index and as a category have delivered 5-year return of around 26%. Since active funds in India so far have outperformed the stock indices by a significant margin, index funds have not been popular and therefore, have a very low level of assets under management.

Equity Funds for Tax Planning

These are also known as Equity Linked Saving Schemes (ELSS) and qualify under section 80C. Investments in these funds lower the taxable income by a maximum of Rs. 100,000. These have a lock in period of three years. Their returns have been impressive and provide a very good avenue for tax exemption combined with high returns. Their 5-year returns have been very close to the average of large cap diversified funds around 41%. HDFC Tax Saver and Prudential ICICI Tax Plan have performed well with 5-year returns of almost 55%.

Sectoral funds

These funds have the mandate to invest in a specific sector. Some of the Indian sectoral funds are:

- Auto
- Banking
- FMCG
- Pharmaceutical
- Technology
- Infrastructure

In general, their performance has not matched the other funds with 5-year returns around 30-35%. Moreover, in each sector, getting good 15-20 liquid stocks might be problematic. So these funds might have a high concentration in 2-3 stocks and thus suffer from higher risk, less choice and illiquidity.

Exchange-Traded Funds (ETFs)

These are innovative and new instruments. These are portfolios of securities, usually of well-known stock indices but increasingly of industry-sector and country indices, that trade like individual stocks.

ETFs are very successful in many markets abroad and are getting more popular gradually in India. ETFs are currently available on Nifty, Nifty Junior, Sensex, and the Banking Index.

Taxation

Taxation on Stocks in India is one of the most favourable in the world.

Equity Funds

Contributions

Contributions to a specific class of funds known as Equity Linked Saving Schemes (ELSS) are eligible under Section 80C. These reduce taxable income by a maximum of Rs.100,000 in one year. Investing in other stock funds does not qualify for this exemption. ELSS, unlike other stock funds, have a lock-in period of 3 years.

Earnings

Earnings from Stock Funds come either in the form of dividends or capital gains. Dividends have a taxation rate of zero. Short-term capital gains (units held for less than 1 year) are taxed at 10% while long-term capital gains (units held for more than 1 year) have zero taxation.

Maturity Amount

Principal amount on redemption does not attract any taxation. This is applicable even to ELSS, although it saved tax on the principal amount at the time of investment.

Direct Equity

Taxation treatment is completely similar to equity mutual funds. Contributions to certain specified stock issues reduce taxable income under Section 80C. Securities Transaction Tax is applicable for both stock funds and direct equity transactions.

Making taxation so favourable just shows that there is a real intent towards channelizing domestic savings towards equities and augurs well for Indian equity market, going ahead.

Conclusion

Rahul realizes that stocks are the absolute top strikers. They dominate all other asset classes in terms of real returns globally and consistently over long periods of time.

In the short run these could be volatile, but in the long run they are very stable. It will be fair to say that, contrary to popular perception, a diversified stock portfolio held over a reasonable period of time has minimal risk.

This is the asset class which makes a real difference in wealth creation. Therefore, it should be an integral part of every portfolio. However, to realize their immense potential, the three principles of Valuation, Time Horizon, and Diversification, as described in this chapter, should be followed.

Courtesy: PTI

Courtesy: The New Indian Express

Adam Gilchrist and Mahendra Singh Dhoni: exciting and versatile contributors

Chapter 9

Real Estate- The Wicketkeeper Batsman

Selecting his team, Rahul is glad he understands how best to utilize his top strikers. He then turns to his other players. Who among them is an absolute imperative and should be selected next...

Real estate plays a dominant role in total wealth; and housing is by far the biggest expense. For most people the purchase of a residence is the biggest and one of the best investment decisions they make in their entire lives. It not only satisfies the basic need for shelter but can also provide tremendous capital appreciation.

It is a very interesting asset class where decision-making is not based on financial aspects alone. There is a big psychological component to it and it evokes lots of emotions and images. Lots of family disputes and Hindi movie scripts can be attributed to this asset class. In *Deewar*, when one brother claimed that he had Ma (mother), the other brother disdainfully said that he had a bungalow. Although it was the other way around, the point is made that bungalow occupies an important place in an individual's psyche.

Moreover, any unfavourable development can cause the value of most asset classes to fall, but real estate at that time goes up. For example, rampant inflation can cause a decline in both stocks and bonds, but real estate might actually go up. Consequently, real estate's role as a part of a multi asset portfolio is very important in reducing the risk while at the same time increasing the portfolio yield.

Real estate is versatile and multifaceted; and fulfills multiple roles. If self-occupied, it provides safety. If rented out, it gives you liquidity. If bought for pure returns, it enhances your portfolio yield.

Multi-tasking real estate can be compared to a good wicketkeeper-batsman as both have multiple roles. Many teams, like siblings for property, will fight to have a competent wicketkeeper who is a good batsman too. A wicketkeeper with fine abilities behind the stumps can save a tremendous number of runs. If he is a good and reliable catcher and stumper, his team feels safe. If he happens to be a good batsman also, then the probability of his team winning multiplies manifold. Adam Gilchrist is one such example and he is one of the most important factors for Australia's dominance. Some teams might prefer to *rent*, like Rahul Dravid in his wicket keeping stint for India, to conserve other resources like batting. However, many experts believe that not having a specialized wicketkeeper is to the detriment of the team. Now of course Indian team has a genuine wicketkeeper batsman in Mahendra Singh Dhoni and it has made a tremendous difference to the team's fortunes.

October 31, 2005, Sawai Man Singh Stadium, Sri Lanka vs. India - The Battle of Wicketkeepers

One batted for 50 overs, scored 138 unbeaten and kept wickets for 46 overs. Another kept wickets for 50 overs, batted for 46 overs and remained unbeaten on 183. For Sri Lanka's wicketkeeper batsman Kumara Sangakkara, it was a mixed day. A belligerent

Mahendra Singh Dhoni who won the battle of wicketkeepers by a mile, reduced what looked like a match winning knock, to mere statistics.

Sri Lanka batted first and scored an imposing 298 for 4 in their 50 overs. Along with Sangakkara's 138, Jayawardene contributed 71 runs. India had an atrocious start, losing Sachin Tendulkar in the first over itself. That brought in Dhoni and he together with Sehwag started dominating the bowling immediately. They took the score rapidly to 99 in the first 15 overs. Dhoni continued to dominate the bowling in spite of India losing Dravid and Yuvraj. He ended the match with a six in 46.1 overs itself. His amazing 183 was scored in only 145 balls with 15 fours and 10 sixes.

India finally had found a wicketkeeper batsman - a match winner in its portfolio.

Advantages of Investing in Real Estate

- It satisfies one of the most basic human needs - the need for shelter.
- It can produce a rental income or if self-occupied, saves on rent
- It can also appreciate in value and provide capital gains. Globally, over a long time horizon, it produces a good risk adjusted return.
- It satisfies psychological needs like pride in owning one's own house, overcoming the fear of not having a roof over your head and sense of control, so much so that you can even put a mirror on your bedroom ceiling. Besides, holding a big physically visible asset assuages lots of nerves.
- It provides financial leverage—this is defined as the use of borrowed money to buy an investment with a larger value. When an individual can invest borrowed money and earn

a rate higher than the rate of interest payable on the loan, the financial leverage is profitable. Traditionally, real estate investors borrow from 60 to 80 percent of the value of the properties they acquire, which is a much higher leverage ratio (of loan to asset value) than is available on most other forms of investment.

- Investors benefit from tax laws that encourage real estate ownership. These are described in detail in the taxation section of the chapter.
- Real estate provides a good inflation hedge. While other assets might lose value with mounting inflation, this can actually gain in value at that time.
- It has low correlation with stocks and bonds, which makes it very valuable in any portfolio.

Risks of Investing in Real Estate

- Market risk - prices can fluctuate and can be very volatile.
- Property destruction and cost of replacement - there could be natural calamities, which could destroy the property.
- Developer risk - developer might not live up to his promises. Also title deeds could generate disputes. Many tenants refuse to vacate the property.
- Structural flaw - termites, leaky basement or roof, shifting foundations are some that could cause sleepless nights.
- Changes in neighbourhood quality - an actress might move to the neighborhood or the government suddenly decide to develop an international airport there. On the negative side, a garbage dump might come up in the vicinity.

- Low liquidity, high transaction costs - an asset will be considered liquid if it can be sold easily without lowering costs. Real Estate has comparatively low liquidity. If it were to be sold in a hurry, say at a time when the economy is depressed, the investor might have to settle for a much lower price.
- Financial risk - if a house loan is financed on a floating rate.
- Landlord's duties-these could be onerous.

Distinctiveness of Real Estate

- Value is not only financial but also psychological
- Investment decision is of concentration rather than diversification. Big chunks of the portfolio are invested in one or very few units. Diversification in this asset class will be possible when real estate funds are introduced.
- Each unit is distinct, unlike stocks and bonds. For example, one unit of Infosys is similar to another. Two investors having 300 stocks of Infosys have identical positions, but their real estate positions when both own one housing unit each, could be very different.
- Unit can only be liquidated in one big chunk; thus comparative liquidity is much less.
- Transaction costs are much higher; thus, further impacting liquidity.
- Ideal time horizon for investing in real estate is much longer than even stocks.
- There is no Exchange where there is uniform price discovery. Each transaction has its unique characteristics.

Table 9.1: USA Comparative Returnsand Risk 1994–2006

Investment	Averagerate of return in %	Risk–Std. Deviation in %
Residential Real estate	10.53	4.44
Farmland	14.03	11.06
Business real estate	10.78	2.77
Common stocks	9.62	19.71
Corporate bonds	7.51	13.92
Small stocks	21.96	28.11

Note: This shows that over a time horizon of 12 years, Real estate showed very good returns with low risk (volatility or standard deviation). These are USA statistics but provide a good indication about the favourable return/risk performance of real estate

Placing of Real Estate in Portfolio

There is a very clear distinction between buying property for self-occupation and buying it for investment purposes. Therefore, these would be placed in different sections of the portfolio.

This distinction is important for decision making, since for self-occupation, one might be prepared to pay more, knowing full well that prestige or restricted supply is causing a property to be overvalued. Moreover, the returns have to be compared against comparable "safe" instruments. However, when real estate is used

Table 9.2: Placing Real Estate in your Portfolio

Needs	Instruments	Percentage	Return
Liquidity			
Safety	Real Estate for self-occcpation		
Yield enhancing	Real estate as an invesdment		

Source: Finance Doctor

for enhancement of yield, sensitivity to projected returns should be very high and here the comparison is with other high yielding investment avenues.

Beneficial Role of Real Estate in a Portfolio

Real estate has an interesting relationship with stocks and bonds. For example, current conditions are such that the expected GDP growth rate is 8-9%, corporate earnings are healthy, individual incomes are booming and interest rates are stable at a lower level. These conditions favour stocks as well as real estate. However, the same conditions are not conducive for a healthy bond market. Therefore at this point of time real estate is positively correlated to stocks and negatively to bonds.

However, these correlations, whether positive or negative, break down frequently. For example, if there is any unfavorable event whether in the form of a major geopolitical event or a terrorist attack, stocks and bonds might go down. But real estate, given its physical tangibility, might even go up in value. In other words, 'flight to safety' under difficult conditions might favour real estate and that is one of the main reasons why this asset class occupies such an important position in any individual portfolio.

However, portfolio analytical studies show conclusively that addition of real estate to a portfolio comprising stocks and bonds is very beneficial. Total portfolio returns increase while the volatility (risk) of the portfolio decreases. This is because real estate has a neutral to slightly positive correlation with stocks and a neutral to mildly negative correlation with bonds.

Real Estate Valuation

As with any other asset, price for real estate comprises certain fundamental factors combined with unique demand/supply dynamics of property.

Physical factors

- Land
- Construction material
- Labour

Psychological factors

- Pride in owning
- Physical tangibility of the asset
- Prestige in an area, locality or even a specific unit
- Control
- Fear that a particular area will be out of reach in the future

Demand and Supply

The market for real estate is different from the market for cars and carrots. When real estate demand goes up, matching supply movement is at a sluggish pace. Houses take time to build and also might face the following constraints:

- Zoning/Planning laws or permission to build – regulation might be due to environmental constraints, or existing owners might be thwarting additional construction.

Whatever the reason might be, this 'regulatory tax' could be a very hefty component of property prices.

- Controlled release of stock: a developer might do it in phases to get a better price.
- Limited supply of suitable land in a particular city, area or a compound.

Income stream

For pricingof any asset, one of the most useful factors is the income stream it generates. For stocks, earnings per share and its relation to the price (P/E ratio) is the most widely used indicator. Similarly, for property, its ability to generate rent gives a good idea of the price. Rental yield will be annual rent (R) divided by the price (P) and is a very beneficial ratio. This has to be combined with the potential of capital gain.

Equilibrium of Buying and Renting

Since housing fulfills a basic need for shelter that can be satisfied by either buying or renting, observing the equilibrium between the two gives a good indication of whether a particular property is over priced or under priced.

If the decision is to buy, the buyer has to make a down payment and because of the possible leverage, he borrows money where he has to pay EMI (equated monthly installment). Each EMI payment is a combination of interest on the loan and repayment of principal. For simplification, we will take the EMI as if the entire amount was being financed. Buying will entail additional expenses like real estate taxes, utility payments, home insurance, and repairs and upkeep. However, there will be savings in the form of income tax reduction. We will designate the net cash outflow for the homebuyer as E.

Alternatively, if he rents the same property, he pays rent , and this we will designate as R.

The difference between two alternatives is that by paying E, he also gets to own the asset. Market forces will keep E and R in equilibrium. If house prices soar and interest rates rise to give a very high E and if R is depressed, E-R invested elsewhere over the same time frame, can give rise to an amount greater than the asset value. Then people will start preferring renting rather than buying. Price will come down and rents will become more till the equilibrium changes again.

E/R ratio for a property over a period of time and also on a comparative basis with other properties is very useful for determining the pricing status.

Real Estate Valuation Cycle

Like any other asset, real estate also goes through price fluctuations, which overshoot as well as undershoot away from its fairly-priced value. Therefore, there are periods when it is very attractive to buy real estate, and there are times when it is overvalued.

What causes these fluctuations? We saw how stocks and bonds are connected to the economic business cycle. Real estate also is connected but with a major difference. With each unit being unique, superimposed on the general business cycle are demand-supply curves of a city, area, sub-area, housing compound and eventually the individual unit itself.

To understand this player and cycle better, Rahul considers an actual example of a major township:

Valuation Example: Gurgaon Story - Development of a Township

Gurgaon falls in the state of Haryana, just on the outskirts of southern Delhi. South Delhi had acquired a very prestigious status with the elite generally preferring to live there. Real estate values there had skyrocketed. By the late 1980s, however, the colonies were getting congested there.

First Phase 1988 to 1992 - Initial Launch

Given this backdrop, various concerned agencies decided to aggressively develop the Gurgaon area, and acccorded prominence to the location and naming it 'best address south of south Delhi'.

They planned a township characterizing it as an Information Technology park and one that is self-sufficient with its own commercial area, shopping, schools and health-care facilities.

Initially, with a bit of active marketing and attractive low prices (since at that time Gurgaon was perceived as remote), it attracted early adopters who saw potential in investing there and also some end users.

Second Phase 1992 to 1996 - Surging Prices

Thus a bit of hype got created about the investment potential of the new area and the prices went up. Additionally, the economy started doing better post-reforms, non-resident interest in India grew and a powerful positive real estate cycle kicked in. The investment element and the prestige factor gave it an extra boost. The developers here induced a heavy dose of regulatory premium by releasing the stock very gradually. Consequently, the prices just surged although there was very little actual development.

Third Phase 1996 to 2003 - Falling Prices

The situation was now one in which little occupancy and low rents were combined with high prices. Investors begin taking their profits while end users took their own time in moving. The price-rent ratio was astronomical. Also, looking at the high prices, the developer took steps to increase supply. Simultaneously, the general business and economic cycle began cooling off. This was exactly the reverse of the initial scenario and the market just tanked.

Fourth Phase 2003 to November 2006 - Rapidly Escalating Prices

The market remained depressed for many years and it took another economic expansion to lift it. Meanwhile, the supply of residential units was going up with a lag time. Major companies set up their offices, and end users (residents) started moving in. Important facilities like schools and hospitals started getting constructed. Smart shopping malls and glizy multiplexes appeared on the scene. The area was living up to its potential. Rents were going up because of more people moving in while the property prices wre still static. Our price/rent ratio was going down rapidly, eventually making it attractive for people to buy.

Moreover, interest rates in India started getting aligned with global rates and came down. EMIs based on low housing prices and low rates declined at a rapid rate. EMI to monthly rent ratio (E/R) became very low. The economic growth started picking up and the stock market zoomed up in 2003. Still, surprisingly, the prices remained depressed. Psychologically, the people still remembered the hit they had taken when the prices had declined.

Finally, there was a major surge upwards in 2004. The trigger came in the form of a major highway being announced linking the airport to Gurgaon. Prices rose dramatically,even increasing 3 to 5 times in a span of 12 - 18 months.

Lessons from Gurgaon - Importance of Customized Research in Real Estate

Rahul saw that the real estate pricing cycle is influenced by many demand-supply factors specific to a particular area. Moreover, for an investor, real estate transaction is a single, concentrated unit transaction and is a substantial part of his portfolio. Therefore, an investor in real estate has to be very careful. Extensive, unique, customized research going down to the unit level is essential.

Unlike stocks, there is no exchange for discovering a uniform price, which is communicated to all the participants. A buyer and a seller have to determine a price after negotiating with each other. Therefore, gathering and owning information is essential.

Also the motivation of different sellers could be different. Somebody might be trying to sell in a hurry. In an overvalued area, there still might be very good deals. Eminently successful real estate investors believe that finding a motivated seller is more useful than even a good location.

Therefore research has to be individualized and intensive in the area. You have to know a bit of history of that area. You have to talk to residents; you have to talk to brokers. Since bid-offer spreads are so high, going to some brokers as buyer and some as seller will be very useful. This is of course in addition to looking at the general business cycle.

You have to see the rental yields and their past history. Also a comparison with similar properties will be useful. A comparison of EMI to Rent will also be helpful. Here also looking at the past history and comparing similar properties is beneficial.

This can result in identifying tremendous opportunities. For example, one very striking thing from our Gurgaon story was that prices remained depressed for so long, although it was evident from residential and commercial development that it was realizing its potential. In 2003 it was easy to forecast that prices are going to go up tremendously. While the surge in 1994 was on hype and potential, the surge in 2004 was on actual realization of that potential. When it moved, it jumped at a very brisk rate and returns were astronomical.

The Gurgaon story also shows that the real estate market is very cyclical and the participant has to be very careful, like in all other asset classes. As the prices go up, developers find it attractive to release supply. With a lag time, when there is sufficient supply, demand might be cooling off because of high prices. Therefore, boom and bust in real estate could be pronounced.

Some Important Issues in Real Estate

Buying vs. Renting

Overall, real estate makes a very fine long-term investment especially when it is intended for own useage. We have already discussed non-financial reasons, which motivate a person to buy. Purely on financial reasons, it is very beneficial to add real estate to the portfolio.

In the safety section, real estate returns over a period of time are much higher than other safety assets like RBI bonds and post office schemes. Besides, it reduces the risk of portfolio with its diversification ability.

Renting is beneficial only infrequently. Certain circumstances are good for the makeshift wicketkeeper:

- When frequent transfers are possible;
- When somebody does not have time and inclination for upkeep, repairs and other hassles;
- When real estate is in a grossly overvalued stage of its cycle.

Astronomical Returns - Perception or Reality?

We many times hear that an old uncle invested Rs. 50,000 in a home in 1955 which is now worth a crore in 2005. On an annualized compounded basis, the return is 17%. It is the great power of compounding that produces a very good absolute value. Housing, because of its relative illiquidity and big transaction costs is a long-term forced savings programme. Important, as compared to other safe savings, its long-term returns are higher and therefore it is a fine investment.

However, purely for investment purposes, its expected yield has to be compared with other assets. Real estate, undoubteadly in certain areas, has been a top performer; but Indian stocks have also performed admirably well. For example, equity funds like Franklin Bluechip have provided a compunded annualized return of 29.1% over a span of 13 years, implying that an investment of Rs. 10 lakh made in December 1993 would be worth Rs. 2.72 crore in December 2006. It is imperative that principles of investing in real estate should be rigorously applied.

Principles of investing in real estate, which is not for self - usage:

- Long-term horizon, in the range of at least 10 years
- Comparison with other long-term assets like stocks
- Valuation - thorough monitoring of the property cycle.
- Intensive localized search.
- Careful scrutiny of legal documents and developer's past record.

Taxation.

There are significant tax concessions on an own occupied house. Interest on loan up to Rs. 150,000 can be deducted from taxable income. Also under recently enacted Section 80C, payment of Rs. 100,000 for repaying house loan principal is also a deductible.

Capital gains are classified as short-term when the property is held for less than three years and long-term when the property is held for more than three years. Short-term capital gains are taxed at marginal rates. Long-term capital gain is taxed at 20% rate, although cost is adjusted for inflation. They are exempt if the capital gains are invested back in the property or alternatively under Section 54EC dealing with Capital Gains tax, these can be invested in designated bonds like REC bonds where the lock in period will be three years.

New Development - Real Estate Mutual Fund

In June 2006, the Securities and Exchange Board of India (SEBI) approved the guidelines for Real Estate Mutual Funds (REMFs). REMFs shall initially be closed ended and will have a lock in period. The schemes will be listed on the stock exchanges and their NAVs will be declared daily. REMFs shall appoint custodians who shall safe keep the title of real estate properties held by the fund.

REMFs will invest directly or indirectly in real estates. Their investment options include direct purchase of real estate property, inestment in mortgage (housing lease) backed securities, equity and debt instruments of companies dealing in properties or undertaking real estate development.

REMFs have multiple benefits. These will provide an easy way for the investor to participate in the healthy returns of real estate - one of the best asset classes as we discussed in the chapter.

Investors can thus avoid the cumbersome process of buying, maintaining and selling real estate. They just have to follow the same simple procedure of filling up a form and signing a cheque, similar to what they do presently for equity and debt mutual funds.

It will also enable the small investor to allocate part of his portfolio to real estate. He could not get involved earlier because of high entry costs. Minimum unit size is likely to be a very small amount.

It provides good diversification and therefore, will be beneficial for reducing the risk of the portfolio as a whole. Additionally, concentrated risk of investing in one particular property will also be avoided since the asset management company will invest in properties throughout the country and in different categories like residential and commercial properties.

Overall, it will provide a healthy avenue for investors to construct a portfolio with greater returns at a lesser risk.

Conclusion

Rahul realizes that real estate is a very versatile asset. When intended for personal use, owning it under most circumstances is the correct decision. It makes a very fine long-term investment. It increases the return on an individual's portfolio while reducing the risk at the same time. Also it does well under unfavorable circumstances like high inflation, when other assets falter. Therefore, it is a favored asset class.

However, when bought for enhancing yield, its projected return should be compared carefully against other assets. Its relative illiquidity and high transaction costs should also be taken into account.

It is a big asset bought and sold in a single deal. Moreover, its price is not only governed by general economic factors but also by local factors. Therefore, intensive research focusing on history of rental yields (past history and present comparisons to other properties, areas) is very useful. It helps in spotting tremendous investment opportunities while avoiding glaring mistakes.

Confident that his wicketkeeper will be a Gilchrist/Dhoni incarnate, Rahul steadily journeys towards victory.

Courtesy: PTI

Shivnaraine Chanderpaul - Defending well under stressful conditions

Chapter 10

Debt - Steady Batsmen Providing Stability Under Difficult Conditions

Rahul reflects that like business cycles, cricket innings have contrasting phases which have to be navigated. The objective should be to put up as many runs as possible while at the same time preserving wickets. There are stages when a hostile bowler is bowling or suddenly a couple of good batsmen get out in quick succession. Sometimes, the pitch itself is not conducive to stroke play and runs have to be accumulated patiently. At that juncture, a batsman who is steady and can provide stability to the innings is required. Besides, if he has the capability to add runs, even though at a slower pace, it is very beneficial.

Each team generally has one or two batsmen of this genre. It is important to note that these players have a high degree of

Table 10.1: Steady and Stable Performers

Player	Average runs per innings (consistency)	Strike rate-runs per 100 balls (risk)
S. Chanderpaul	36.63	69.87
Marvan Atapattu	37.8	66.97
Mohammed Kaif	33.01	72.6
Michael Vaughan	28.36	68.41

consistency although a lower strike rate than Stock players. Their utility to the team is high and many times, they contribute to the team's victory.

Debt provides a similar steady role in a portfolio. Long-term studies of returns of different asset classes in various countries show that its returns are lower than those of stocks and real estate in the long run. However, it provides a stabilizing effect to the portfolio, especially when economic conditions are tough.

Debt, simply stated, is a borrower taking money from a lender with an agreement to return the principal at a pre specified time. In between, he pays interest on the money borrowed at periodic intervals. As it is just borrowing and lending money, Debt is a very broad asset class with a wide range of instruments extending from simple products like bank deposits, provident fund, post office schemes, national savings certificate to complex instruments like zero coupon bonds.

Debt securities are sometimes called Fixed Income Securities because in most cases they pay contractually fixed, periodic interest payments that cannot vary during the life of the security. However, there can be variations like floating rate debt agreements, but the important consideration is that the benchmark for variable rates is also pre-defined.

While stocks are wealth builders, debt instruments are wealth preservers. These have two fundamental properties that make them a very important part of any portfolio. First, they provide steady income, sometimes with tax advantages. Second, they often, though not always, move in opposite direction to that of stocks. For example, bond prices typically go up when the government reports an increased unemployment rate. Difficult economic conditions causing erosion in stock prices are when bonds do well; and this inverse correlation helps the portfolio chugging along during various stages of the business cycle.

February 9, 2003, Cape Town, South Africa West Indies vs. South Africa, World Cup Match

This was the first match of the 2003 World Cup. South Africa were the hosts and the home crowd was expecting a victory, not only in this match but the cup itself. There was palpable excitement in the whole country for this inaugural match.

West Indies won the toss and elected to bat. Shaun Pollock, South Africa's hugely talented captain, opened the bowling and got both openers, Chris Gayle and Wavell Hinds, out very cheaply. West Indies were reeling at 7 for 2 in 6 overs. At this stage, looking for runs aggressively would have been suicidal. Brian Lara and Shivnarine Chanderpaul had to negotiate very difficult conditions and provide stability to the innings. They defended well for the next 24 overs and took the score to 109 for 2. Then with only 20 overs left and 8 wickets still standing, they unleashed their aggressive batsmen.

Lara changed gears completely and along with Hooper, Powell and Sarwan took the score to 278 for 5, adding 169 runs in the last 20 overs. Lara got a well-deserved century with 116. South Africa in reply started well and were 79 for 1 in 16 overs. However, they were under pressure chasing 278 and kept losing wickets at regular intervals. Finally, they ended at 275 for 9, just 3 runs short. This proved to be one of the most exciting matches of the World Cup.

Chanderpaul's strike rate in this innings was only 56.7, but was extremely valuable in providing stability. When the situation was tough, like a good debt instrument, he provided stability and safety, and at the same time produced runs, although at a slow pace.

What are Bonds?

Bonds are the most familiar kind of debt security. A bond is merely an agreement between a borrower and a lender stating the terms of a loan. A lender (the bond holder) agrees to advance a certain amount of money (principal) to a borrower (bond issuer). In exchange, the borrower agrees to repay the loan in full at some future date (maturity), as well as to pay a certain amount of interest periodically (yield). A bond holder receives a fixed interest payment each year until the bond matures. This payment is known as the coupon because most bonds used to have coupons that the investors clipped off and mailed to the bond issuer to claim interest. At maturity the debt is repaid. The amount that is repaid is known as the bond's face value, par value, or maturity value.

Illustrating with an example, the Indian government issues Rs.1 lakh 10-year bond in January 2005 with a yield of 6% and a semiannual coupon. This means the owner of that bond (lender) has lent the government Rs.1 lakh. The owner can expect the government to repay that Rs.1 lakh at maturity in January 2015. Over the ten years, the owner of the bond will receive Rs.6000 annually, in two semiannual installments of Rs.3000 each.

Types of Bonds

There are numerous varieties of bonds. Categorization is done in many ways, but the most useful is based on two important factors:

- Credit Worthiness of Issuers
- Maturity - there is a wide range from thirty days to fifty years.

Some major categories are:

- **Government bonds** also known as Treasuries or Gilts, are issued by the government and have zero default risk. They have a very large range of maturities.

- **Corporate bonds** are issued by corporates. Credit worthiness of corporates will vary and is a very important factor. The more credit worthy a borrower is, the less interest he has to pay.

Different rating agencies like Moody's Investors Service, Standard & Poor's, and CRISIL assign credit ratings to various organizations. This facilitates determination of the interest rate for a specific borrowing company.

How do Bond Prices Move?

Bond prices, like stocks, move up or down depending on prevailing interest rates. Changing credit worthiness of the issuer also alters the bond price. Thus, there is a possibility of capital gains or losses.

The following illustration demonstrates how the theoretical price of a bond will move with changing interest rates:

Suppose an issuer issues a 10-year bond of Rs.1000 paying a coupon of 8%.

The buyer of the bond gives the issuer Rs.1000 for a bond with Rs.1000 face amount. In exchange, he expects to receive Rs.80 each year and the principal amount of Rs.1000 at the end of 10 years.

Now assume that soon after the bond is issued, inflation rises more than expected. Bonds have a secondary market and the bond holder can sell it. However, other investors are worried about inflation and will not be satisfied with an 8% income stream. They want a higher interest rate, but the bond's coupon of 8% is fixed. The solution lies in the new bondholder paying less than Rs.1000 so that his effective interest rate rises automatically. Thus, the old bond holder realizes a capital loss.

Therefore, an inverse relationship exists between the price of a bond and interest rate/yield. Simply stated, as interest rate increases, bond price falls; and if interest rate decreases, bond price rises. For a longer-term bond with plenty of remaining fixed interest payments, effect of interest rate movements on bond price today will be even more pronounced. This relation has an important bearing on asset allocation of a portfolio since interest rates are an integral part of the the business cycle.

How does an Investor Get Returns?

Bonds have two types of income:

Interest income

The interest income on any bond when it is issued is determined by several factors. By far the most important determinant is inflation or, more accurately, inflation expectations. Bonds that are issued with high yields come out when investors are particularly worried about inflation; those that are issued at relatively low yields are sold when inflation outlook seems tame.

A second major determinant of the yield on a bond stems from the credit worthiness of the issuer. An investor is taking more risk and therefore looks for a higher return from a less credit worthy issuer.

Capital gains/ losses

As illustrated in the preceding example, bond price fluctuates with changing interest rates. Especially for long-term bonds, capital gains or losses can be fairly pronounced.

What Risks Does an Investor Face?

Credit risk

Issuer of the bond, the borrower, will fall on hard times and not be able to keep paying interest or return principal when the bond becomes due, often after a long period. A bond issuer who cannot repay principal or who stops paying interest is said to have defaulted. Credit/ default risk explains the large difference in yields on bonds of the same maturity that are issued by different entities, ranging from the relatively low rates offered by the U.S. Government, which is assumed to have no risk of default, to the very high yields on bonds issued by ailing companies (often called junk bonds) and governments of emerging markets.

Interest Rate Risk

As we saw earlier, Bond prices are sensitive to interest rate movement.

Reinvestment risk

It can be significant when the holding period is long. The risk affects reinvestment of interest payments and also principal amount available when the bond matures.

Liquidity risk

Liquidity is gauged by the ease with which an asset can be converted to cash. An asset is considered to have high liquidity when it can be sold easily without lowering the price. Many times, a particular issue of a bond might not find a liquid market. Even if a bondholder has read the market well and wants to adjust his position, he might find a much more unfavourable price than what prevailing interest rates warrant.

Debt Funds - Best Way to Invest in Bonds

For a retail investor, buying or selling bonds is much more cumbersome as compared to stocks. Reasons are multiplicity of issues, illiquidity, high bid/offer prices and less transparency and uniformity.

The best way to invest in bonds for a retail investor is through Debt Funds that are mutual funds investing in bonds.

Types of debt funds

Debt funds can be classified along two dimensions:

- Maturity: short, medium, and long
- Credit quality: low, medium, and high

All debt funds will be a combination of these two dimensions. Some common types of debt funds available in the market are:

Gilt funds

These funds invest only in bonds issued by the government and that is where the name Gilt (extremely reliable instruments) comes from. Since government has zero risk of defaulting, credit quality of gilt funds is of the highest order.

Maturity could be variable since the government issues a wide range of debt paper. Depending on average maturity, Gilt funds can be classified as long-term, medium-term, or short-term.

Long-term Gilt Fund is useful for capital gains in a declining interest rate environment.

Income funds

These are debt funds, which can invest in both government and corporate bonds. Their flexibility in both maturity and credit quality can produce all sorts of permutations. For example, we can have a medium-term income fund with high credit quality or an income fund that is long-term with medium credit quality.

Liquid funds

Liquid funds are debt funds that invest in debt securities with an average maturity of 90 days. These are useful parking vehicles for short-term surpluses. These earn returns a little more than bank deposits and at the same time have zero market risk, offering a high degree of safety.

Floating rate funds

These debt funds comprise securities, which have interest rates pegged to a benchmark rate. For example, a security might be paying an interest rate equivalent to 6-month inter-bank offered rate.

These funds are useful when interest rates are rising steadily.

Hybrid funds

These funds have varying degrees of stocks and debt securities. Monthly Income Plans comprise 80% debt securities and 20%

stocks. While this heavy proportion of debt produces steady income, the 20% stock component adds to a good monthly return.

Another popular hybrid is Balanced Funds with 65% stocks and 35% debt. The debt proportion smooths the volatility of fund returns. With the 65% stock proportion, balanced funds manage to retain the more favourable taxation treatment of stocks.

Taxation of Debt Funds

Contributions

These are not eligible for any tax deduction.

Earnings

Earnings are in the form of dividends and capital gains with the distinction between short-term and long-term gains being based on the duration of one year. Dividends are free from taxation in the hands of the investor. However, Mutual Fund Company pays a dividend distribution tax of 25%, which affects the fund's NAV and therefore indirectly, the investor is paying this tax. Short-term capital gains tax is taxed at investor's marginal taxation rate, while long-term capital gains at 10%.

Maturity Amount

Principal amount is not counted as part of taxable income on redemption of investment.

Conclusion

Debt comprises all instruments that involve borrowing and lending and is a broad asset class. Because of its fixed return feature, it lends safety and stability and is a very useful and integral part of every portfolio.

A very useful feature of this asset class is that it does well under tough economic conditions which are not conducive for stocks and real estate. Although its returns are lower, it provides a very useful avenue for asset allocation in specific business cycle stages.

Essentially, bonds are wealth preservers while stocks are wealth builders. While stocks should be the core of any long-term portfolio, bonds are a second essential ingredient. In an overall investment portfolio, bonds play the role of the control rods in a nuclear reactor, tempering the speed of the reactions to keep everyone safe but not slowing them so much that no energy is produced.

Courtesy: Pradeep Mandhani/imageallsports.com

Shaun Udal - 39 years old England spinner, considered to be over the hill but sometimes useful

Chapter 11

Small Saving Schemes - Players Over the Hill?

Introduction

Rahul's thoughts turn nostalgic - every player, however great he might have been in his prime, goes through the same cycle. He makes his debut, establishes himself and seems invincible and irreplaceable at a certain point in time. However, time does not wait for anybody. The same player eventually enters a phase where retaining his place in the team becomes difficult. He is competing with new young players whose skills are consistent with the new environment.

The game of cricket has changed a great deal. Shorter version of the game with 50 overs a side was introduced only about 35 years ago. It was only in 1975 that the first world cup (of one day internationals or the shorter version of the game) was played. Now the rate of change is even faster. Who would have thought that we would be seeing a world cup of an ultra short version of the game (matches of only twenty overs each innings) in the not too distant future?

It was only 25 years back that Dhirendar Sehwag was given an opportunity to showcase his talent. The national coach was aghast to see the footwork and the slash shot over the third man's head going for a six - the coach could see no more and rejected the applicant summarily. His son Virender, an exact replica, is now one of the most exciting players on the international cricket scene.

The skill set required to succeed in the shorter game is more flexible. The batsmen who were regarded very well in the past had a copybook style with a straight bat and a solid defense. Now the ability to improvise, not to let go of any scoring opportunities, to have a wide repertoire of strokes including unorthodox ones and much higher fitness levels are the desired attributes.

It was in 1958 that the Government of India set up the National Savings Organization headquartered in Nagpur. It was controlled by the Ministry of Finance and the objective was to encourage household savings and to assure a good safe return to people. It provided people with a good avenue for earning healthy and very safe returns on their savings.

For quite some time, the returns on these savings schemes remained attractive. These were much higher than the prevailing inflation rate, thus providing a good real return. But then the winds of change appeared on the horizon. The Indian economy was finally shedding its self-imposed shackles. Interest rates had to move in tandem with the global economy and came down significantly. Maintaining small savings rates at a much higher artificial level was increasingly, an unsustainable proposition for the government. Small savings rates had to be aligned with prevailing interest rates, as much as possible.

Simultaneously, with the higher economic growth, other asset classes started giving much higher rates. For example, in the year 2005-06, while Public Provident Fund, Post Office Monthly Scheme and Government Savings Bond generated 8%, Diversified Stock Funds provided 75% and Real Estate was also booming.

December 21. 2005, Rawalpindi Stadium, England vs. Pakistan

It was the fifth match of the series with Pakistan leading 3-1. England was playing to uphold their prestige. They batted first and got off to a disastrous start. Very soon, they were 21 for 2 in six overs with Mohammad Asif bowling very well. Solanki and Flintoff provided some stability to the innings. But England kept on losing wickets regularly and ended with a meager total of 206 for 9 in its 50 overs.

England took the field and in walked its 39-year-old spinner, Shane Udal, who had made his debut in 1994 against New Zealand. In the past 12 years, he had played only 11 matches with a very undistinguished record. His utility was obviously perceived to be low, but he was specially brought in on this tour to capitalize on the slow and spinning wickets of the subcontinent.

Pakistan coincidentally were also 21 for 2 in 6 overs, but Yasir Hameed and Mohammed Yousuf had a great century stand and took the score to 122 for 2. With only 85 runs required and 8 wickets in hand, the result seemed to be a foregone conclusion. Here Udal provided an important breakthrough, getting Yasir Hameed out with a ball that turned and jumped. This wicket initiated a collapse and Pakistan lost an exciting match by six runs.

Udal again was very useful when England squared the test series against India by winning the third test match in Mumbai. He took 4 wickets (including Tendulkar) for 14 runs. He was promptly dropped for England's next match against Sri Lanka. However, nobody was surprised since that was being played in totally different conditions in England.

Udal illustrates the story of small savings schemes - over the hill in most circumstances, but can be useful in certain special situations.

Small Savings Schemes

There are different kinds of small savings schemes with varying eligibility criteria, investment amounts, tenors, returns, liquidity/ withdrawal rules, and tax treatment.

1. Public Provident Fund (PPF)

Eligibility

Any individual can subscribe in his own name or on behalf of a minor for whom he/she is a guardian. Each individual can hold only one PPF account. NRIs are not permitted to open PPF accounts. Similarly, HUFs are not permitted with effect from May 13, 2005. However, accounts already opened shall continue until maturity.

Amounts required

The scheme promotes regular savings by ensuring that contributions are made every year to keep the account active; these contributions can vary from Rs. 500 to Rs. 70,000 per annum.

Returns & Tenor

It presently offers a return of 8% annually and runs over a 15-year period. The rates have been aligned more and more towards the market rates and the government has the flexibility to revise the rates in either direction. Returns along with principal are paid on maturity.

Liquidity/ Withdrawal

A subscriber is permitted to make one withdrawal every year from the 7th financial year onwards of an amount not exceeding 50% of the balance at the end of the 4th year immediately preceding the year of withdrawal or at the end of the preceding year.

Taxation

The invested amount is eligible for deduction under Section 80C. Total maturity amount including the principal and interest is absolutely free from taxation.

2. Employee Provident Fund (EPF)

Eligibility

EPF is a retirement benefit scheme, available to salaried employees.

Amounts required

A stipulated amount (currently 12%) is deducted from the employee's salary as a contribution to the fund. The employer also contributes an equal amount to the fund.

An employee can contribute more than the stipulated amount if the scheme allows for it. However, the employer is not obligated to match the additional amount.

Returns & Tenor

It presently offers a return of 8.5% annually. Here, the rates have also been aligned more and more to the market rates and the government has the flexibility to revise the rates in either direction.

The amount accumulated in EPF is paid at the time of retirement or resignation. Or, it can be transferred from one company to the other, if one changes jobs. In case of death of the employee, the accumulated balance is paid to the legal heir.

Liquidity/Withdrawal

Premature withdrawal is possible for certain reasons like daughter's wedding or buying a home. Taking a loan is also possible upon fulfilling certain conditions.

Taxation

Invested amount is eligible for deduction under Section 80C. The total maturity amount, including principal and interest amount is absolutely free from taxation.

Premature withdrawal is not taxed if an employee has worked continuously for five years, not necessarily with one employer. Even for less than five years, there is no taxation if health reasons have caused a disruption.

3. Post Office Monthly Income Scheme

Eligibility

An individual on his own behalf or on behalf of a minor or a person of unsound mind of whom he is the guardian may open an account.

Amounts required

Minimum amount is Rs. 1,000 while the maximum amount is Rs. 300,000 in a single account and Rs. 600,000 in a joint account.

Returns & Tenor

It presently offers a return of 8 % annually and payment is made every month. The maturity period for deposits under the scheme is 6 years.

Liquidity/ Withdrawal

Withdrawals are permitted after one year at a 2 % discount and after three years at 1% discount. Withdrawals after 3 years are permitted without any deduction.

Taxation

Investments in Post Office Monthly Income Scheme are not eligible for any tax benefits. Interest income on these deposits is part of 'income from other sources' and is taxable.

4. Post Office Time Deposit Account

Eligibility

An individual on his own behalf or on behalf of a minor or a person of unsound mind for whom he is the guardian may open an account.

Amounts required

Deposits can be made in multiples of Rs. 200. There is no upper limit on the investments.

Returns & Tenor

The investment can be made for 1 year, 2 years, 3 years, or 5 years. Returns are dependent on tenor, annualized returns being 6.25%, 6.5%, 7.25%, and 7.5% for 1, 2, 3, and 5 years respectively.

Liquidity/ Withdrawal

Withdrawals are not permitted before 6 months. No interest is payable if a deposit is withdrawn after 6 months but before 1 year. If deposits made for 2 years, 3 years, or 5 years are prematurely withdrawn after one year, interest will be paid at a rate 2% less than the rate applicable to the period for which the deposit has run.

Taxation

Investments in Post Office Time Deposits are not eligible for any tax benefits. Interest income on these deposits is part of 'income from other sources' and is taxable.

5. National Savings Certificate (VIII Issue)

Eligibility

Any adult individual can purchase National Savings Certificate (NSC) in his or her name or jointly with another adult individual. Besides, parents and guardians can also purchase them on behalf of a minor. NRIs cannot invest in NSC (VIII Issue).

Amounts required

Any individual can subscribe to the scheme with a minimum investment of Rs. 100. There is no upper limit on investment in this scheme.

Returns & Tenor

The rate of interest is 8% per annum compounded half-yearly, payable on maturity. A certificate shall mature after 6 years from the date of certificate.

Liquidity/Withdrawal

Premature encashment of certificate (any time before 6 years) is allowed under specific circumstances only, such as death of the holder(s), forfeiture by the pledgee or under court's order. No interest is payable on encashment within one year. After one year and before three years, simple interest is payable at the post office savings bank's rate of 3.5% for the completed months only.

Taxation

Deposits made in this scheme qualify for tax deduction under Section 80C of Income Tax Act subject to an upper limit of Rs.100,000. Interest on these certificates is taxable on accrual basis.

6. Kisan Vikas Patra

Eligibility

Any adult individual can purchase Kisan Vikas Patra (KVP) in his or her name or jointly with another adult individual. Besides, parents and guardians can also purchase them on behalf of a minor. NRIs are not permitted to invest in KVP.

Amounts required

There is no upper limit in this scheme and individuals can invest any amount they wish. The minimum investment required is Rs.100.

Returns & Tenor

The scheme matures in 8 years and 7 months and carries a return so as to double the money during this period. For example, if an individual buys a certificate of Rs. 1,000, he will receive Rs. 2,000 on maturity. Effectively, he is earning a compounded annualized return of 8.41%.

Liquidity/Withdrawal

Premature encashment within 2.5 years is allowed under specific circumstances only such as the death of the holder or under court order. No interest is payable on encashment within one year. Between 1 and 2.5 years, simple interest is payable at 3.5%. After 2.5 years, encashment is more flexible and the rates more favourable.

Taxation

Interest on KVPs is taxable on accrual basis.

7. 8% Savings Bonds (Taxable)

Eligibility

Any individual in his own name or jointly with another individual or on behalf of a minor or HUF may purchase these bonds.

Amounts required

Minimum amount is Rs.1000, while there is no upper limit.

Returns & Tenor

It pays 8% annualized. Interest amount is payable at half-yearly intervals or compounded half-yearly and paid cumulatively, at the option of the subscriber. It matures after 6 years.

Liquidity/Withdrawal

The bonds are not transferable and loan facility is not available.

Taxation

Interest income, as the name suggests, is taxable.

8. Senior Citizens Savings Scheme

Eligibility

The scheme is available for citizens above 60 years of age. Individuals above 55 years may invest if they have retired at superannuation. NRIs (Non-Resident Indians) and HUF (Hindu Undivided Family) are not permitted to invest in the scheme. An account may be opened singly or jointly with a spouse.

Amounts required

The maximum amount allowed is Rs.15 lakhs.

Returns & Tenor

Deposit earns interest of 9% per annum. Interest is payable every quarter on 31st March, 30th June, 30th September, and 31st December of each year.

The scheme has a duration of 5 years.

Liquidity/Withdrawal

A depositor may close the account and withdraw the deposit at any time after the expiry of one year from the date of opening the account. However, a deduction of 1.5% shall be made if the account is closed before two years and 1% if the account is closed after two years.

Taxation

The interest income from the scheme is taxable.

Conclusion - When are these schemes useful?

Small saving schemes are designed to be long-term in nature with fixed returns and with penalties for early withdrawals. They are therefore utilized for meeting long-term financial goals like retirement or children's education.

However, in recent times their returns are being aligned with prevailing interest rates and just slightly above inflation. Thus, the real returns offered by these products are inadequate and do not fulfill the objectives of the investor. Moreover, comparative returns of competing asset classes are much higher. Besides, as we have seen in the earlier chapters, risk posed by asset classes like stocks and real estate is minimal if used in the right manner.

With the advent of packaged retirement products like pension ULIPs, there is flexibility where an investor can also allocate retirement funds to stocks. Moreover, favorable taxation treatment is no longer applicable to only small savings schemes. It extends to a gamut of products including Equity-Linked Saving Schemes. All these factors combined make the lustre of small savings schemes much less appealing.

However, there are certain situations where these products are useful. For example, matching contributions in Employee Provident Fund (EPF) makes it very attractive.

Additionally, some of the schemes are effective when a very safe periodic income stream is required. For example, Senior Citizens' Savings Scheme with its high assured return is very beneficial. At a lower percentage but for the same reason Post Office Monthly Income Scheme is also useful.

Rahul chuckles as he recalls how Udal steered England to victory. He realizes that over the hill players need not be just dismissed and confined to cobweb-covered musty record books. In certain circumstances and if judiciously drawn upon, they can prove beneficial.

Courtesy: Pradeep Mandhani/imageallsports.com

Mohammed Kaif - Good protection is essential for winning

Chapter 12

Insurance – Absolutely Necessary 12th Man

Introduction

Rahul's thoughts turn philosophical — how unpredictable a cricket match can be. How many times teams have snatched defeat from the jaws of victory — all because of one unforeseen development, one error. In a match that is all but sewn up, an important batsman perishes to a silly shot jeopardizing the outcome of the match. Or the opponent's batting is under pressure but a fielder drops an easy catch, giving the opponents an extra lease of life while snuffing life out of his own team.

A cricket innings is very similar to life's journey. Sometimes it starts very well only to flounder later or it could be the other way round. Even if one has made a huge fortune, preparing for unforeseen events is essential. A team that has prepared for contingencies can wriggle out of tight situations.

Everybody encounters a broad range of risks as they go through life. A comprehensive risk management program is essential and a necessary part of effective wealth management. Rahul generally places one of his best fielders at Cover and sometimes finds it beneficial to go for Extra Cover too.

February 6, 2006, Arbab Niaz Stadium, Peshawar, India vs. Pakistan

This was a very important match for India. They had just lost an important test series and were looking for redemption in the one-day series. It was the opening match of the one-day series and important to start on a winning note.

Pakistan won the toss and put India in to bat. Their decision seemed vindicated when they got Sehwag out very early. However, Sachin was in good form and Pathan again played his role as No. 3 batsman to perfection. He scored 65 in 65 balls and got out in the 16th over with the total at 99 for 2. Dhoni walked in and had a rollicking partnership with Sachin. They scored at the rate of 7 runs per over for the next 18 overs; and when Dhoni got out in the 34th over, India's score was 225 for 3. With Yuvraj and Sachin, the momentum was maintained and by the end of 42 overs India was in a winning position at 285 for 4.

Here the mistake happened; complacency set in. India had amassed a huge fortune and it was bound to win. Nothing could now change the result, which was a foregone conclusion. They did not go for just those extra 10-15 runs that would have INSURED their victory.

Sachin was very close to his century, which he duly achieved in the 45th over. The score was 305 for 4 in the 45th over with Sachin and Dravid batting. Commentators were sure of at least 40 runs in the last 5 overs. Surprisingly, India could add only 23 and ended at a total of 328.

Although it was still an imposing total, the last 5 overs had swung the momentum in Pakistan's favour. Instead of a dispirited team, their batsmen walked in with plenty of swagger. First 8 overs produced 50 runs and only then did they lose their first wicket. The second wicket partnership was big and swift. Salman Butt and Shoaib Malik took the score to 201 in only 32 overs, trimming the target drastically. Pakistan eventually won comfortably in spite of losing wickets regularly.

A dejected Dravid in his post match conference lamented that only if we had secured just a few more runs, the result would have been different. We have frittered away a huge fortune.

Insurance Definition

Insurance is providing protection against a possible event causing financial loss. The most common form is Life Insurance, which protects beneficiaries against loss of earning capacity of a breadwinner. Insurance is a financial risk management or more precisely, a risk transference tool.

Risk Identification

Everybody has to identify what risks he should protect himself from. What should he buy insurance for? One simple way is that wherever financial loss can be significant and it will be difficult to replace the asset, insurance should be bought. Some such significant risks are:

1. income earner's life – risks are death, disability, and critical illnesses affecting earning ability

2. income earners' and family members' health- risks are costly medical treatment

3. home risks are burglary, fire, floods, etc.

4. car risks are theft, damage, and liability

Types of insurance

1. Life insurance
2. Disability and Critical Illness insurance
3. Medical Care insurance
4. Property insurance
5. Auto insurance

Life Insurance

Concept

Insurance company is the entity that assumes this risk and for taking on this risk, the insurance buyer pays a premium to it. The company collects money from multiple buyers and pays from this pool, those for whom the risk actually materializes. With the help of detailed studies, insurance companies have a fair estimation that when they sell 100 policies, how many they would have to honour in a given period of time; and that becomes the criterion for determining average premium.

Types of Life Insurance Policies

Whatever name an insurance product is called by, essentially there are two types –

- Pure protection policies: these are known as term insurance policies. Here the policy provides only protection and there is no payback of premium. The advantage is that a small amount of premium can provide a significant life cover.
- Combined protection and savings policies - An insurance company collects premium, utilizes part of it to provide life cover and invests the rest. Endowment, Whole Life, Money-

back and ULIPs (unit linked insurance policies) are all combinations of savings and protection. Except for ULIPs, all other savings and protection policies generally invest in government and other high-grade bonds, and have therefore, given lower returns.

ULIPs (Unit Linked Insurance Policies)

Unique feature

As the name suggests, the saving part of the premium is utilized to buy units in a way similar to that of mutual funds. Additionally, choices for the buyer are more extensive; units could be bought in alternative investments with various combinations of stocks and bonds.

Examples of alternative ULIP investments (nomenclature will differ for various companies):

- Maximiser - equity-related, equity could be 100% and debt not exceeding 25%
- Balancer - mixed with equity not exceeding 40% and a minimum of 60% debt
- Protector - debt at a maximum of 100% and cash not exceeding 25%
- Preserver - debt at a maximum of 50% and cash at a minimum of 50%

ULIP Costs

Part of premium paid is deducted upfront as administrative charges. Administrative charges are on the higher side especially in the initial years. In the first year, most companies charge 10-15% of premium. These come down steadily; for example, 3% in 2nd and 3rd years and 2% in 4th and 5th years.

Additionally, there are life cover (protection) charges which like any other insurance policy are dependent on age, health status, and amount of cover. Finally, there are fund management charges.

ULIP Comparative Returns

In the 3 years from 2002 to 2005, ULIPs with 100% equity earned 27% on a compounded annual basis against an average return of 41% for comparable diversified stock funds. Similarly, balanced ULIPs earned 18% against a return of 31% for balanced mutual funds.

Should Protection be Combined with Savings?

The question that always arises is whether one should combine protection and savings in one product or think of these needs separately and buy distinct insurance and investment products. My recommendation is to treat insurance and investment products separately for the following reasons:

1. Pure protection cover costs very little and by not masking it with superimposed investment, the buyer buys the right amount of insurance cover which he really needs. Same premium, if mixed with an investment element, might make the person grossly underinsured. For example, one might be paying an annual premium of a lakh but only a small proportion might be allocated to actual protection.

2. Administrative charges of insurance companies are high especially in the initial years. So the money actually invested becomes much less. Whatever a buyer pays for life cover in a term policy is also deducted for providing a similar cover in the combined product.

3. Actual returns of insurance investment have not compared well with those of comparable mutual funds.

4. Taxation benefits of insurance products can be replicated very easily. Equity linked savings schemes also qualify under section 80C and have the same benefit of reducing taxable income by a maximum of Rs.100,000. Money received on maturity of an insurance policy are free from tax. Similarly, a long-term capital gain on stock funds (if held for more than 1 year) is tax-free.

Buying the Right Life Insurance Policy

Initiating the process of buying a policy, Rahul is deluged with calls from agents of various companies. He finds it increasingly difficult to find the best company and policy. Amount of insurance cover suggested varies from one advisor to another; as does the premium to be paid for different schemes. He comes across multiple terms like endowment, money back, term assurance. Agents bring brochures and computer printouts showing numbers difficult to understand. They tell him about guaranteed additions, annual bonus, and reversionary bonus.

The following five points will help decision-making:

1. **Determining the amount of life insurance cover required:** A good thumb rule is 'total monthly expenses multiplied by 150'. For example, if monthly expenditure is Rs.30000, then life cover should be Rs.45 lakhs. This lump sum would generate a monthly sum sufficient to meet expenses.

2. **Cutting through the jargon of multiple products and schemes:** There are lots of products in the market with different nomenclatures. As stated earlier, the buyer should concentrate on pure protection and should ask the company representative how much premium he is paying for each lakh of life cover. By concentrating on only protection element, he can also easily compare pricing of various companies.

3. **How much premium to pay?** Premium depends on factors like age, health status, and duration of insurance. Being aware of indicative rates will give Rahul a good idea of premium to pay. For example, for a pure protection policy, a 30-year-old has to pay annual premium of about Rs.290 for Rs.1 lakh cover for 25 years. A 35-year-old will pay about Rs.400, while a 40-year-old will pay Rs.580. If the cover is for 30 years, the 30-year-old's premium increases to Rs.330; for a 35-year-old, it is Rs.460. Individual health status will modify these indicative rates.

   A 35-year-old person can buy the requisite cover of Rs.45 lakhs with only Rs.18000 annual premium for a pure protection policy.

4. **Differentiation among various companies:** Insurance is a long-term product. Besides pricing and efficient processing of initial policy, elements of after-sales service like amendments, reminders about due premiums, documentation, promptness are important in choosing the company. References of existing customers should be asked for.

5. **Critical illness insurance as an adjunct to life insurance:** Protection for critical illnesses like cancer, renal failure, heart attack, coronary artery bypass graft surgery, major organ transplant, and stroke could be added. Critical illness cover is similar to life cover, in the sense that it covers the same risk of 'earning person's capacity to earn' being affected. It is distinct from healthcare insurance that covers medical costs of hospitalization.

Medical Insurance

This is an Absolute Necessity

With increasing longevity, an individual's medical expenses can put a serious dent in his expenses. Hospitalization for a major illness can be very costly. As medical services improve and get privatized, an individual will have to budget for such expenses.

Product is Becoming Better

More companies in India are offering health insurance with additional features and wider coverage. Customers have a better choice.

Product Features

Cost

Premium is dependent on age and health status. For a 30-year-old with a lakh of coverage, annual premium is around Rs.1200. For a 40-year-old, the cost will be higher around Rs.1700 for a lakh.

What does the Policy Cover?

It covers healthcare expenses for a condition that requires hospitalization for more than 24 hours, generally. Some advanced technological procedures that require less than 24 hours of hospitalization are also covered by some policies. Insurance company will also reimburse pre-hospitalization and post hospitalization charges based on actuals with maximum of coverage amount of the policy. Of course, there will be certain exclusions like pre existing conditions and some other specified conditions.

Treatment will have to be undertaken in designated hospitals, but exceptions are made when an emergency might necessitate otherwise.

Rewarding Loyalty

If an individual is with an insurance company for a number of years, the company might cover some pre-existing conditions and exclusions will become less. For example, joint replacements might become permissible if the person has bought insurance for three consecutive years. Moreover, coverage might be extended in the older age group, although initiating a medical policy for the first time after a certain age might not be possible.

Renewal

There is an option to buy either a one year or a two-year policy, and then an individual will have to go for renewal. Above 45 or 50 years, medical tests might also be required.

Cashless claims

With the advent of third party administrators, it is possible to avail cashless service. This is much better than paying on your own first and then awaiting reimbursement.

Taxation benefits

Under section 80 D, taxable income is reduced by a maximum of Rs. 10,000, or Rs. 15,000 for a senior citizen.

Floater Policies

The whole family could be covered in one policy where total family coverage amount is specified but no individual limits are ordained. For example a family of 3 takes coverage for 3 lakhs; it is possible that all 3 lakhs are claimed for one family member's medical expenses.

Insurance for Other Risks Including Property, Household Effects, Vehicles and Other Possessions

The principle remains the same as for life and medical insurance. For any insurance, the same risk management exercise has to be used:

1. Risk identification: what could happen?
2. Risk evaluation: where could such an event leave me?
3. Risk control: how much coverage should I opt for? Replacement value should guide the value of coverage taken.

Conclusion

Insurance is important for guarding against unforeseen events that can put enormous pressure on an individual's finances. It is essential since no other product can deliver protection against such risks.

Major risks have to be identified and evaluated. Life insurance is one of the most important risk protection tools. It is beneficial to buy the requisite cover, and term insurance policies enable that with their affordable premium.

For policies with savings element, so far their return and cost performance are inferior to those of comparable pure investment products. Consequently, the verdict is that insurance is like an absolutely necessary 12th man – the team is incomplete without his protection expertise. However, his run-making ability is still suspect and he will have to do better to force his way into the playing eleven.

Courtesy: PTI

Rahul Dravid has held the innings together and led the team to victory many times

Chapter 13

Retirement Planning – Sheet Anchor

Introduction

Rahul is perplexed. He's put together a great team, and yet he doesn't feel very confident. With the impending cricket season just around the corner, he is still a worried man. Is this a great "team" or a team of "great players"? He unhappily recalls instances in which, in spite of some great individual performances, the team did not win. There were good opening partnerships, but typically, after getting off to a blistering start, the openers got out when apparently well set. He analyzes various factors and hones in on the main one - there was nobody visualizing the end goal and holding the team together around it. There was no proper planning of the innings in totality. Nobody was taking the responsibility as a finisher.

Musing, Rahul realizes that it is imperative that somebody plays the sheet anchor role and others rally around him. They should not be in a situation where they start well, but lose their way and end up requiring 55 runs in the last 5 overs with 3 wickets in hand. They have to visualize the end goal much better.

Similarly, retirement is the culmination of all wealth related planning. There is no point having periods of extravagance only to be anxious when income inevitably starts dwindling. Retirement by definition is the period that has no active income.

Retirement planning is intimately connected to basics: to the way Rahul defines wealth - a person is wealthy if his passive income is sufficient to sustain a desirable lifestyle. In some ways, it involves constantly striving to increase the proportion of passive income that eventually becomes 100% of total income.

November, 28. 2005, Wankhede Stadium, Mumbai, India vs. South Africa

It was a tough match for India - the final of the series and India were 1-2 down. Dravid and Chappell were aware that the recent resurgence of the team and their flexibility to experiment with innovations would be severely compromised if they were to lose this series.

India won the toss and elected to field. Surprisingly, they were gaining a reputation for being good chasers - a delightful change from being described as good chokers. It was a difficult pitch and Pathan made good use of seaming conditions to make early inroads into the South African innings. However, they recovered to end at 221 for 6 with the help of a fine innings of 91 from Jacques Kallis.

India had a bad start losing Gambhir and Sehwag early; and Rahul Dravid walked in at a dismal score of 46 for 2. From the very beginning, Dravid built and paced his innings with the end goal in sight. Tendulkar also got out when the score was only 83. Thereafter, first Yuvraj and then Dhoni returned to the pavilion; but Rahul did not run out of steam and determinedly soldiered on. He played the role of sheet anchor to perfection and finally took the team to victory in the 48th over. Dravid scored 78 not out in 106 balls and was obviously the man of the match. Although Sehwag's 27 in 20 balls was like an investor making 100% return on one stock in one good year, it would have been of little use without Dravid resolutely holding the innings together and eventually ensuring victory.

Retirement Planning

Definition

It is essentially the matching of income being generated presently to meet the needs arising later. It involves taking a part of today's resources and income, earmarking them as retirement assets and investing them appropriately, with the ability to generate periodic returns sufficient to take care of post retirement needs.

Environment - Onus on Individuals

The prevalent major trend is to put the onus on individuals to provide for their retirement needs. Moreover, this trend will continue to strengthen even further. This is because of the following factors:

- Lifetime employment is steadily going down.
- Increasing longevity.
- Movement from joint to nuclear family.
- Defined benefit to Defined contribution.

While the others are rather obvious, 'defined benefit' and 'defined contribution' are part of jargon currently bandied around, and Rahul is a little hazy about what they actually mean.

Defined Benefit

Here post-retirement benefit is already defined and automatically accrues upon retirement. Retirement benefits depend on how long somebody has worked for the organization and his remuneration and job level at the time of retirement. Different organizations have different methods of setting up pension plans and they have to honor this pre-determined payment. Consequently, defined benefit puts tremendous strain and generates huge pension liabilities for organizations, including government.

Defined Contribution

Defined contribution as the name suggests, defines the contribution that an employee has to make to his retirement plan. Then the employer also contributes a pre-specified amount to the employee's retirement plan. The employee then decides where to invest this amount among various alternatives available to him. The amount ultimately generated will depend on the quality of investment decisions; and two individuals with totally identical contributions can end up with very different retirement amounts.

Worldwide there is a trend of moving from defined benefit to defined contribution for the obvious reason that it does not create a huge unmet pension liability for employers.

Steps for Retirement Planning

As the onus of retirement planning lies essentially on the individual, it is imperative to take steps towards this end. These have been elaborated in Chapter 6 and include:

a. Visualizing a retirement lifestyle vis-à-vis current lifestyle

b. Estimating number of years left for retirement

c. Estimating retirement expenses in today's money

d. Estimating future inflation — CII inflation table helps us

e. Estimating future taxation rate on post-retirement income

f. Calculating amount of lump-sum required at time of retirement

g. Calculating required real rate of return that needs to be generated on earmarked retirement assets

We can get into detailed calculations but an easy rule of thumb simplifies matters. The key is to save every month an amount equivalent to around 15-20% of current monthly expenses and to generate a real return of 9-10% on it. This results in achieving the goal of a retirement lifestyle comparable to the current lifestyle. Therefore, in a matching plan, an employee contribution of 10% with an equal contribution from the employer is sufficient.

Here the assumption is that the investor has initiated saving 20 years prior to retirement; for example, at the age of 40 years assuming retirement at 60 years. Power of compounding is such that if he starts just a bit earlier, required amount of earmarked funds goes down dramatically. For example, if he has 25 years, the amount required is only half; he needs to save only 8-10% of current monthly expenses compared to 16-20% with 20 years left.

Retirement Planning Products - Two Types

Essentially, retirement planning has two dimensions – first of building up the corpus during one's income earning phase; and second, of generating a periodic income flow from this corpus after one retires. There are arrays of products available for satisfying these dimensions.

The numerous ads on television flash through Rahul's minds – the upright patriarch, shoulders back, head held high, providing for his progeny even after retirement; the high-flying corporate employee tossing aside his demanding job to paint, to fish, to live life king-size; the provider bringing a wide Cheshire Cat grin to his wife's face as he buys a far larger home than she had ever imagined. Rahul comes out of his reverie to delve deep into these alluring products.

1. For Building up the Retirement Amount

A. Provident fund

A detailed description is already in the Chapter on small savings. Essentially, it suffers from very low returns of only 2% above inflation, which might be even lower in the future. These are much below the required real rate of return. By relying on Provident fund, one will lose the game.

B. Pension plans

Pension plans are offered by insurance companies to help individuals build a retirement corpus. These are packaged and designed to perform all the retirement steps.

Simple pension plans

They collect regular periodic payments (premiums), invest these payments in government securities and bonds, and generate a sum of which at least 2/3rds has to be invested in annuities for producing periodic income. Their major drawback is that like the Provident Fund, they produce low returns, hardly beating inflation.

Pension ULIPs – Unit-linked plans

These are far more flexible than simple pension plans, the main difference being that the investor has a choice to invest in stocks too. Pension companies provide various alternatives with allocation to stocks in different proportions such as:

a. Conservative - investing only in bank deposits and money with zero allocation to stocks

b. Balanced - allowed to invest up to 60% in stocks

c. Aggressive - with 100% allocation in stocks

There could be further shades in between.

Characteristics of Pension ULIPs

a. Flexibility - they provide considerable flexibility by allowing frequent switches between various alternatives. Depending on the provider, a number of switches might be absolutely free every year. They also allow increases in premium (top-ups) and even reducing, stopping, and restarting the premium. Additionally, redemption after 3 years is without any surrender charges.

b. Taxation Advantages - Premium up to Rs. 1 lakh is allowed as a deduction from taxable income under Section 80C. Further, maturity amount is tax-free. However, periodic income generated from the lump sum is taxed at investor's marginal tax rate.

c. Returns - ULIPs have delivered good returns on an absolute basis with Aggressive or Growth option (100% allocation to stocks) earning about 45% return (average return of top 10 pension ULIPs) between Jan. 31, 2005 and Jan. 31, 2006. However, this pales in comparison with the average return of 65% of top 10 diversified equity funds during the same period – i.e., about 20% higher.

d. Costs – These are very high especially in the initial years. For example, one company's administrative charges are as high as 22% in the first 2 years. This significantly reduces the amount really invested. However, from 3rd year onwards, charges drop to only 1%.

e. Restriction - pension plans have a restriction that on maturity, 2/3rds of the accumulated amount has to be invested in one of the available Annuities (described later in the chapter).

C. Customized Retirement Solution

A customized solution can easily be structured which retains the advantages but eliminates the drawbacks of Pension ULIPs. This can provide higher returns at lower costs. This is structured by combining stock and debt mutual funds. There are multiple mutual funds available which combined together can provide a desired composition.

An investor can do it himself or with the help of a good financial planner or a wealth manager.

Example

An investor earmarks the funds for retirement and invests them in a desired proportion. For example, if the business cycle and personal conditions warrant a balanced allocation, he can invest 60% in stock funds and 40% in debt funds.

2. For Generating Periodic Returns Post-Retirement

Once a good retirement amount has been accumulated, on maturity, it must provide a periodic return. Products to facilitate this are:

A. Annuity

Investor pays a lump sum (purchase price of annuity) and receives a periodic payment. Period is predefined and could be anything like monthly, quarterly, or yearly. Buyer of annuity is known as an Annuitant.

Types of Annuities

There could be various types of annuity products depending on their duration and whether purchase price is returnable or not. Some examples are:

Lifetime annuity without return of purchase price

Annuitant continues to receive periodic payments during his lifetime and purchase price is not returned on his death.

Lifetime annuity with return of purchase price

Annuitant continues to receive periodic payments during his lifetime and purchase price is returned to his nominee on his death. Of course, the periodic payments will be less than the first alternative.

Lifetime annuity guaranteed for a certain number of years

Here even if the annuitant dies, the nominee will keep on receiving the periodic payments for a pre specified number of years, for example 20 years. If the annuitant survives this period, he continues to receive the payment for his lifetime. This annuity can also be with or without return of purchase price.

Last survivor annuity

This could be purchased by a couple in which if one dies, periodic payments will continue for the lifetime of the surviving spouse.

Future variable annuity products

Annuities suffer from the disadvantage that even if a good retirement sum has been accumulated, if interest rates are low at the time of retirement, the retiree might receive a much lower than expected monthly income. In many countries, annuity products in which returns are linked to inflation are available. If prevailing inflation is higher, a higher rate compensates the annuitant.

Even more interesting are annuities, where a certain floor rate is guaranteed and in addition to that returns are related to a specified index. For example, to an assured return of 5%, the appreciation percentage of a specified stock index like Sensex is added. This results in the retiree participating in a stock rally and having much more remunerative senior years.

B. Senior Citizen Saving Schemes

This is a scheme applicable to citizens above 60 years and in certain situations for people above 55 years of age in which they have taken voluntary retirement. Features of this scheme are:

Minimum amount	Rs. 1000
Maximum amount	Rs. 15 lakhs
Tenor	5 years
Return	9% annualized
Payment period	every quarter

Premature encashment— possible after one year but with penalty. If it is before 2 years, 1.50% of the amount must be paid. If 2 years are completed, then a penalty of 1% applies.

Taxation— Interest income is taxed as part of the individual's annual income.

C. Small Saving Schemes

There are other alternatives like Post office monthly income schemes, Post office time deposits, and 8% saving bonds that are described in the chapter on small savings. Of course, bank fixed deposits could also be utilized.

D. Customized Annuities

Present packaged annuity products are few and offer low returns. They do not take into account increased longevity where returns are connected to inflation. Some part of the accumulated sum should be invested in yield enhancing assets like stocks. Moreover, these payments are subjected to the marginal rate of taxation.

An annuity-like product could be structured in multiple ways depending on investor objectives. One example would be where 75% is invested in short-term debt mutual funds that produce a regular safe monthly dividend. Rest 25% is invested in high-quality diversified stock mutual fund that produces a good return and keeps the accumulated sum growing at a healthy rate to take care of a long productive life. Also, taxation in such customization is much lower.

Pension ULIPs vs. Customized Retirement Solution -Which is Better?

Overall, Customized Retirement Solution is much better because of the following reasons:

a. Switching Flexibility – It is very similar in both. An investor can keep on varying the proportion between stocks and debt by switching funds.

b. Taxation Advantages – Taxation advantages of Pension ULIPs can be replicated by utilizing Equity Linked Saving Schemes (ELSS). These are specified mutual funds that qualify under Section 80C, thus reducing taxable income by a maximum of Rs. 100,000 in one year. However, these funds have a lock-in period of 3 years - in a way similar to pension ULIPs that have no exit charges upon surrendering after 3 years. Further, the maturity amount is tax-free, since long-term capital gains (if held for more than one year) on stock funds are zero.

c. Returns – Comparative average returns for stock mutual funds and Equity Linked Saving Schemes have been significantly higher than Pension ULIPs.

d. Costs – The entry load is 2.25% of the amount invested for stock funds. However, periodic contributions can easily be structured as a Systematic Investment Plan (SIP) where entry load could be much less. The loads in Pension ULIPs are as high as 20-25% in the first couple of years.

e. Annuity Restriction – Pension ULIPs have a restriction of investing two-thirds of maturity amount in one of the available annuities. Customized solution has no such restriction.

Conclusion

Mulling over it all, Rahul is very clear that retirement planning is imperative for winning the wealth game. This is an end goal that, if not achieved, essentially means losing the war, even if there are periods of affluence and extravagance in between. He must set aside and build up a corpus, akin to Dravid's sheet anchor role of building and consolidating a winning total.

Generating a good real return is the key to effectively utilizing current income for meeting this long-term liability that is bound to arise - it prevents a situation where a frugal current lifestyle is facilitating a good retirement or vice versa. The objective should be a constant good lifestyle. Therefore, the end goal has to be thought of and the earlier one starts, better it is because of the power of compounding.

Rahul recognizes the need for the sheet-anchor, lending direction to his innings in the wealth game - knowing the objective, starting early, investing well. He is confident that all those television ads could be a reality for him. After all, he not only has great players but also a great team.

Courtesy: Pradeep Mandhani/imageallsports.com

Courtesy: Pradeep Mandhani/imageallsports.com

Andrew Flintoff, the multitasking match winner

Chapter 14

Structured Products & Derivatives - Genuine All-Rounders or Bits-and-Pieces Players?

Rahul had a great sense of exhilaration. In this match, they were steamrolling the opposition. He was finally leading a team of 11 players who could all bat like Sachin Tendulkar, bowl like Shane Warne and field like Jonty Rhodes. The opponent batsman slashed the ball hard; it was low and away from him. Rahul, airborne in a totally Jontyesque horizontal position, latched onto the catch and continued to hold it even when falling to the ground with a thud. Rahul woke up with a start; he had just fallen from the bed.

Every captain dreams that all the players in his team are able to bat well, bowl well and field well. However, in reality, most players specialize in something or the other. There are a few who can do everything, but genuine all rounders are very few. Many players with potential to be all rounders end up as bits-and-pieces players who do a little bit of batting and a little bit of bowling.

Some examples of genuine all-rounders are:

Table 14.1: Genuine all-rounders

Player	Average runs per innings	Average Runs per 100 balls	Runs given per wicket (strike rate)	Runs given per over (economy rate)
Imran Khan	33.41	72.84	26.62	3.9
Jacques Kallis	43.93	70.56	32.33	4.83
Kapil Dev	23.79	96.36	27.45	3.72
Andrew Flintoff	34.28	89.16	25.82	4.39

Some examples of bits and pieces players are:

Table 14.2: Bits and pieces players

Player	Average runs per innings	Average Runs per 100 balls	Runs given per wicket (strike rate)	Runs given per over (economy rate)
Clairmonte Lewis	14.38	80.6	29.42	4.44
Richard Illingworth	11.33	56.67	35.3	4.23
D.A. Reeve	24.25	74.81	41.1	4.29

Just like Rahul, every investor dreams that his portfolio is totally liquid, absolutely safe, and generates astounding returns. But the reality is different. Most products are specialists. If they provide liquidity, their returns are low. Similarly, safe products might not be liquid and provide low returns.

Structured products with their flexibility and customization have provided hope by affording multiple benefits. However, many structured products masquerade as genuine all-rounders, while in reality they might be bits and pieces players. An investor should evaluate these products on the three dimensions of liquidity, safety, and returns. Delving deeper is important, specifically in terms of the investor's financial goals. Good quality structured products can make a tremendous difference to a team's fortune as illustrated by the outcome of 1992 World Cup final.

March 25, 1992, Melbourne Cricket Ground, Pakistan vs. England, World Cup Final

It was the day the whole cricketing world was waiting for. The final match of the 5th World Cup was about to be played between the two exciting teams of England and Pakistan. It was a very special day for Pakistan - they had reached the final for the first time, while England were hoping for a 3rd time lucky, having failed in their first two earlier forays into the final stage.

Sunil Gavaskar, as expert commentator, had maintained throughout the tournament that genuine all-rounders and specialists are very important. For him, it was easy to forecast the winner of this final. While England had packed their team with bits and pieces players like Clairmonte Lewis, Richard Illingworth and Dermot Reeve, Pakistan had genuine all rounders like captain Imran Khan and Wasim Akram. For him, it was Imran and Wasim vs. Illingworth and Reeve; therefore, predicting the winner was a no brainer.

Pakistan won the toss and elected to bat. They started badly with openers Aamer Sohail and Ramiz Raja getting out cheaply and they were 24 for 2. Imran had come in at one down and engaged in a long partnership with Javed Miandad. They took the score to 163 before Javed got out. With wickets in hand, they could accelerate. Inzamam made 42 in 33 balls and Wasim 37 in 19 balls, and they ended at 249 for 6 in their 50 overs.

With this kind of score, the match was evenly poised. England started hesitantly - losing Botham for 0 at 6 for 1. Against some accurate and hostile bowling they kept losing wickets and were 69 for 4. Neil Fairbrother and Allan Lamb had a good partnership and took the score to 141, when Akram bowled Lamb with a beautiful swinging delivery. Their bits and pieces players predictably just collapsed in this difficult situation. Finally, England folded up for 227 in 49.2 overs and Pakistan won the World Cup for the first time. Akram took 3 for 49 in his 10 overs.

Unanimously, Wasim Akram with his great all-round performance was chosen as Man of the Match.

Structured Products

As the name suggests, these are products that are constructed from several parts. A structure is made using building blocks, especially derivatives. Structured products are flexible and can be customized to fulfill specific and multiple objectives.

A common example is a capital protected structured deposit; this provides returns that might be related to a stock index, commodity basket, currency pair or any other parameter while the principal amount is totally protected. Deposit returns are linked to a certain condition being fulfilled. For example, returns might be equivalent to appreciation of the Sensex. Another example is if a designated currency pair stays in a pre-specified range for a certain duration, the deposit will yield higher returns.

Because of the flexibility, an unlimited number of combinations can be structured. However, the quality of products is variable, ranging from excellent to completely ineffective. Each individual product will have to be evaluated on its own merits from the perspective of usefulness to the investor.

Most structured products typically employ derivatives. It is therefore beneficial to have basic information on derivatives.

Derivatives - Brief Introduction

'Derivatives volumes in India are now 4 times the stock market volumes' – the headline bewilders a normal retail investor. He knows Indian stock markets are fairly well developed, but what is this new category evoking even greater response from investors? Is he missing out on something that can significantly impact his financial well-being?

In India, futures and options on 31 select shares were introduced in 2001; gradually the list of shares on which derivatives are available has expanded. Investor response has been outstanding and derivatives have overtaken share markets in volumes quickly.

Derivatives, as the name suggests, are not independent but derived from a basic product. They are a contract with a right or obligation to buy or sell an asset at a certain time in the future for a certain price. No exchange of cash and the actual product takes place today. The price of this contract is dependent on fluctuations in the price of the underlying product. The underlying could be anything ranging from stock indices, individual shares, currencies, fixed-income securities, wheat, sugar, gold, silver to even butter, eggs and onions.

Origin of Derivatives

The origin of derivatives lie in agriculture and is illustrated by the following scenes from a popular Hindi movie:

1. *Happy Rural Scene* - Farmers in a coffee-growing village saw the outbreak of a good monsoon. All villagers gathered in the village square, sang happily and broke into a lusty rain dance. The song became one of the biggest hits.
2. *Sad Rural Scene* - Alas, their celebrations were short-lived. Unknown to them, the rain god had been kind in a non

discriminatory way and had provided equal quotas of rain to all the surrounding villages. Supply of coffee ran into a huge surplus and prices collapsed.

3. *Happy Urban Scene* - In the city, a top-level executive of a coffee chain is reaping the fruits of globalization. If Americans can go to Starbucks for an expensive cup of coffee, his nice branded coffee shop in India can be successful too. He has been able to procure his raw material, coffee, at a very low price. He is expecting a huge bonus from his company.

4. *Sad Urban Scene* - However, next year his fortunes nosedived. Coffee crop was not so good and he had to pay exorbitant prices to keep his business going. Market forces didn't allow him any flexibility in increasing the price for his end user.

5. *Happy Rural Urban Ending* - Executive and Farmer are shaking hands. They have just concluded a futures contract - Farmer will sell his coffee at a pre-determined price to the executive at a precise date nine months later. The ceremony was solemnized in an Exchange. Both are obligated to transact at the price mentioned in the contract irrespective of the price prevailing nine months later, and now face no uncertainty. As a side story, Executive's son had fallen in love with Farmer's daughter and they are getting married today.

Futures

This is one of the two main categories of derivatives, the other being Options. Futures' concept remains the same whether the underlying is coffee, a stock or anything else. Stock future is a contract between two entities to buy and sell a specific share at a specific time in the future, at a pre-determined price. It is an obligation and both parties have to transact at that price. Moreover, these are transacted on an exchange that guarantees the trade. Buyers and sellers do not even have to know each other. They just go to the exchange and transact.

For example, an investor enters a futures contract, where he is obligated to buy Infosys at Rs.3200 on Dec. 24, 2005. On that date, if Infosys is trading at Rs.3525, the investor still gets to buy at Rs.3200, thus making a profit of Rs.325. On the other hand, if Infosys is at Rs.3000, he still has to buy at Rs.3200, losing Rs.200. Another interesting facet is that this contract has a very liquid secondary market and can be bought or sold easily. For example, if the price of Infosys in October, much before the expiration of contract, moves to Rs.3415, the investor can sell his futures contract at a good profit.

Moreover, since it is only an intent to buy, the buyer does not have to pay money upfront, and the seller does not have to deliver the underlying. Instead, both the seller and the buyer of futures pay an initial margin to protect against risk posed by movement of the underlying. Initial margin is a fraction of the contract value, depending on the volatility of the underlying. Also, depending on which way the underlying has moved each day, additional margin known as variation margin is either debited or credited to the investor's account.

Options

An option is a contract where an investor has a right to buy (Call Option) or sell (Put Option) a share at a predetermined price, at a predetermined time. The only distinction between Futures and Options is that in an option, the investor has a 'right' rather than an 'obligation'. For instance, he buys Infosys Call Option at Rs.3400, implying he has a right to buy Infosys at Rs.3400 on December 24. If actual price on that date is Rs.3800, he makes a profit of Rs.400. If price is Rs.3200, he does not have any obligation to buy at Rs.3400, unlike in a Future. His option contract just expires worthless. Therefore, an option is similar to insurance where the buyer acquires protection. Seller of that option offers that protection, but at a price. Therefore, akin to insurance, the buyer of an option pays a premium to the seller of the option.

Returning to our Hindi film nine months later...

Sad urban scene – Although faced with no uncertainty, Executive is distressed. Coffee prices have fallen and are much lower than the contracted price. Yet he cannot take advantage of this. Contract apart, he is further hemmed in by the delicate relationship he now has with the farmer – his daughter-in-law would be most upset if he reneges on the contract. Thinking more deeply, he comes up with a perfect solution for the future.

Happy urban scene – Executive has just entered into an option contract with an anonymous farmer through the exchange. Now if the price falls below the contracted one, he is under no obligation to buy and his option can expire worthless. However, if it rises sharply, he can still buy at the lower contracted price. The premium he pays is a small price to pay for insuring his business against huge price rises.

What Explains the Success of Derivatives?

The reasons for its success are multiple. First, it allows investors to invest and take a position with very little money. If a person is bullish on a stock, they can buy a futures contract or a call option by paying only a fraction of what they would pay to buy the same share outright. Secondly, he can express unique and customized views. By buying or selling shares, he can express only directional views. Contrastingly, through derivatives, he can express a view like ONGC shares trading in a narrow range during the next three months. Thirdly, derivatives are useful for hedging. For example, an investor who owned SBI after seeing a rapid up move still feels that the rally is not yet over. At the same time, he anticipates a temporary downward correction. To preserve the gains, he can sell a future or buy a put option.

Construction of a Structured Product

There are various ways to construct a structured product. One common way is to use an option. For example, a 5-year deposit might be linked to Dow Jones Index. A 5-year zero coupon bond of equivalent maturity amount is bought and the remaining money is utilized to buy an option on Dow Jones Index. If the index moves up, this option gains in value thus giving an enhanced return to the investor. In case the index moves down, the option value goes down to zero, but the investor gets his capital back since the zero coupon bond grows into the principal amount on maturity.

Second generation options like range option, knockout, and binary are used to give these products even more customized, flexible, and enhanced features.

Examples of structured products

1. Japanese Stock Index-related deposit

Description

It is a 3-year deposit where the underlying is TOPIX - a Japanese stock index. Deposit returns are related to appreciation of TOPIX, which was at a level of 1400 at inception. Investor gains 1.4 times the percentage appreciation in the index. For example, if the index gains 100% in 3 years, his deposit will gain 140% and become 2.4 times.

At the same time, risk is minimal. His capital is totally protected unless the index touches 980, which is a full 30% away from inception level of 1400. However, if index touches 980, then the investor loses the capital protection and gets a return equivalent to the actual index performance.

This product has a good secondary market and can be sold anytime although the deposit is for 3 years. It is structured using a second-generation option known as knock-out option.

Evaluation on different dimensions

Liquidity - rating is high because of the good secondary market.

Safety - rating is medium. Capital is totally protected up to 30% depreciation of the index.

Yield enhancing - very high rating here, since the investor gains 1.4 times the rise in the index.

Verdict

Real test is to compare it to an alternative product for expressing the same view, for example, a TOPIX index fund. For the structured deposit, the yield enhancing aspect is much better, liquidity is the same and safety is higher. If index goes to 1120, the index fund is losing 280 while this product is protected. If index goes to 2100, the index fund has made 50% while this product has made 70%. If the index goes down to 980, then both lose equally.

Overall, this product is a genuine all-rounder with the ability to greatly facilitate fulfilment of investor objectives.

If we were to have a similar product with Sensex as the underlying and at 10000, it would give 42% return if Sensex moves to 13000 and the investor will not lose anything even if Sensex moves to 7100.

2. British Pound Deposit with a Guaranteed Return of 6% in Two Years and a Maximum of 22% Linked to the FTSE 100

Description

It is a 2-year deposit with British stock index FTSE 100 as the underlying. This deposit guarantees an absolute return of 6% for two years along with the original investment on maturity. The return could go up to a maximum of 22% return over the next 2 years, linked to the performance of UK stock market, namely the FTSE 100 index. A normal British Pound deposit at the time of introduction of this product was earning 9% absolute return for 2 years.

For arriving at the return, the closing value of FTSE 100 at the end of every quarter is taken, and the percentage rise or fall in the index is calculated. A tenor of 2 years will have 8 such quarterly readings. Each reading has an upper or lower limit of 2.75. For example, if the market rises by 6% in a certain quarter only 2.75 will be counted or if the market falls by 5%, only -2.75 will be counted. At the end of the 2-year period, the eight returns (both positive and negative) will be combined, to determine the overall return achieved.

If the calculation produces an overall return of less than 6%, the bank will pay the guaranteed minimum return of 6%.

However, if the calculation produces an overall return of more than 6%, the bank will pay that sum, up to the maximum possible return of 22%.

Evaluation on different dimensions

Liquidity - rating is low. It is a 2-year fixed tenure with no room for liquidity within this period.

Safety - rating is high. Not only is the capital totally protected, but a 6% return is also guaranteed.

Yield enhancing - low, since probability of reaching anything near the maximum is extremely low. In every quarter, the index has to move up by at least 2.75% to give the maximum possible return of 22%.

Stock markets move up in a spiky fashion. There could be situations where markets rise by 6% in one quarter and then fall by 2.75% in the next. So, although the market has moved up by 3.25% overall, the deposit would not have accrued any return over the two quarters.

If we look at the actual movement in this the index for the last 6 quarters, this deposit would have accrued only 5.5%, although index has shown a growth of 12%. This is because of the 2.75% limit and the inclusion of negative returns in the calculation. The probability of beating normal deposit return of 9% is also on the lower side.

Verdict

This product is a bits and pieces player and just masquerading as an all-rounder.

An investor could be very easily misled into thinking that while 6% is guaranteed, at the same time he will be getting high UK stock returns. But in reality, the calculation method limits the upside. Such deceptively good products, if not analyzed well, have a great potential to distort asset allocation and thus, lower the probability of achieving goals.

3. Capital-Guaranteed without Derivatives - a Combination of Debt and Stocks

Description

Insurance companies offer this product where they guarantee the return of that part of premium, which is invested after deducting all expenses. It invests 30% of the portfolio in stocks and 70% in debt instruments. For example, if a total of Rs.100 is invested, Rs.70 will be in debt and Rs.30 in stocks. The portion of Rs.70 even if it returns 6.12% annualised will become 100 in 6 years. By putting a lock-in of 6 years, even if the 30 invested in stocks becomes zero, the insurance company guarantees the return of the invested premium, which is essentially investor's own principal and interest.

Evaluation on different dimensions

Liquidity - rating is low. It has a lock-in period of about 6 years since it has to ensure 70 becoming 100.

Safety - high; since capital is guaranteed in 6 years' time.

Yield-enhancing - low; Since even if stocks do well, total return earned by the investor is still on the lower side. Even if stocks double in value in 6 years, annualized return is only 8.1%.

Verdict

A total bits-and-pieces player not worthy of selection since it has low liquidity, no special safety and poor returns. Even if stocks do well, returns of this product will match a totally safe government small saving scheme with a similar lock-in period with difficulty. Pitfall for the investor is that he could be misled into believing that he will be earning stock-like returns with total safety. On the other hand, a greater proportion of his long-term savings are locked in debt with very low returns. There is tremendous opportunity cost of not investing in assets that produce very good returns in the long term at minimal risk.

Conclusion

Structured products are eminently beneficial with flexibility and customization. They can facilitate achieving an investor's goals by fulfilling multiple needs. For instance, they could combine a high degree of safety with high returns.

Derivatives are the main building blocks for structured products and a basic understanding is beneficial for the investor. An infinite number of permutations and combinations of structured products are available. However, like in cricket, only a few are genuine all-rounders and most are bits and pieces players. It is important for an investor to delve deeper and evaluate these products on the three dimensions of liquidity, safety and returns. This analysis is important - a genuine all-rounder could be a match-winner while bits-and-pieces players could be ineffective and have a huge opportunity cost for the team and portfolio.

These are lifestyle products of the future since they have the capability of ensuring a certain level of income and at the same time enabling participation in the good times. One important example is a retirement annuity product that, in addition to a minimum guaranteed return, offers extra returns benchmarked to a stock index.

Courtesy: PTI

Stuart MacGill - A very useful but still a reserve player

Chapter 15

Alternative Asset Classes – Reserve Players

Rahul is concerned about injuries to a couple of his top players. Additionally, some players are not at the top of their game. He is alert to the reality of too much cricket being played nowadays. Relying on main players to play each and every match is a mistake. For his team to perform consistently, the team has to have good bench strength.

Reserve players have to be nurtured carefully. When called upon, they should be able to step in and perform. For that, they have to be given opportunities in important matches so that they get real experience and develop. Some players, even if very talented, remain on the fringes with minimal deployment. Team management has to think carefully about their role, preparation, and optimal utilization.

Alternative asset classes, by definition, are those which are not in the mainstream. Most investors allocate resources in their portfolios to long-established classes of stocks, debt and real estate and are reluctant to depart from traditional practices. However, there could be circumstances where relying only on the main classes might not be optimal.

Therefore, it is important that investors be receptive. Adding alternatives to the portfolio, at least in certain situations, can be advantageous in terms of enhancing returns while minimizing risk. Two major alternative classes, described in this chapter, are Commodities and Art.

January. 19, 2000, Sydney Cricket Ground, Australia vs. Pakistan

Stuart MacGill is finally making his debut in international one-day cricket at the age of 29 years. He is recognized as the spinner with the best strike rate but worst luck. His misfortune has been to play alongside Shane Warne, recognized as one of the five greatest cricketers of the 20th century.

MacGill has performed well in Sydney and conditions there suit him tremendously. He is expected to do well, but realizes that in spite of good performances, he will continue to get limited chances. He is destined to be a reserve, an alternative, and not a mainstream player.

Australia won the toss and elected to bat. They started poorly and were 23 for 2. Bevan and Martyn performed well under trying conditions, stabilized the innings, and managed to take the score to 286 all out in 49.4 overs. Wasim Akram took 3 wickets for 40 runs.

Pakistan made a brisk start and was 62 for 1 in 8 overs and 100 for 2 in 12 overs, bringing down the required run rate significantly. MacGill was brought on and struck immediately. His first ever wicket in his ODI career was Abdul Razzaq who was going great guns with 40 runs in 38 balls. He bowled superbly and ended with remarkable figures of 4 wickets for 19 runs. Pakistan could not cope with his spin and collapsed for 205 in 45.2 overs. MacGill played an important role in Australia's victory and was rightly adjudged man of the match - one of the most impressive performances by a debutant.

Interestingly, even after such a debut, he played only 2 more one-day international matches with an excellent average of 17.50 and an equally good economy rate of 3.50. However, this reserve player showed his usefulness whenever called upon. When Warne was banned for drug use in 2003-04, Macgill played 11 Test matches and took 53 wickets.

Commodities

Definition

Commodities are the raw materials, natural resources, necessities of life for everybody's everyday life. They are numerous and a few categories are:

Precious metals - Gold, Silver, Platinum, Palladium

Base metals - Copper, Zinc, Aluminium, Tin

Agri commodities - Sugar, Vegetable Oil, Cotton, Coffee, Tea, Corn, Soybeans

Energy sources - Crude Oil, Natural Gas, Heating Oil

Business Cycle & Commodities

Commodities are influenced by the general business cycle. For example, as India continues to grow, per capita income levels will rise correspondingly. This leads to more demand for homes, cars and infrastructure, thus increasing the requirement for commodities like steel, cement, and crude oil among others.

Superimposed on the business cycle are the individual demand-supply cycles of commodities. Commodities, being real hard assets, have pronounced demand-supply cycles. For example, coffee might be in a phase where crop is good, supply is plentiful and demand is average. In such a situation, the price will be on the lower side. A low price will stimulate more demand which will eventually outstrip supply. Prices, therefore, will start moving up. With coffee becoming pricier, suppliers will find it lucrative to increase supplies by devoting more plantation area. However, the lag time for higher supplies combined with increasing demand may lead to a spurt in prices. But high prices will not be sustainable as supply starts kicking in. The cycle of low and high prices will continue.

Figure 15.1: Valuation Cycle

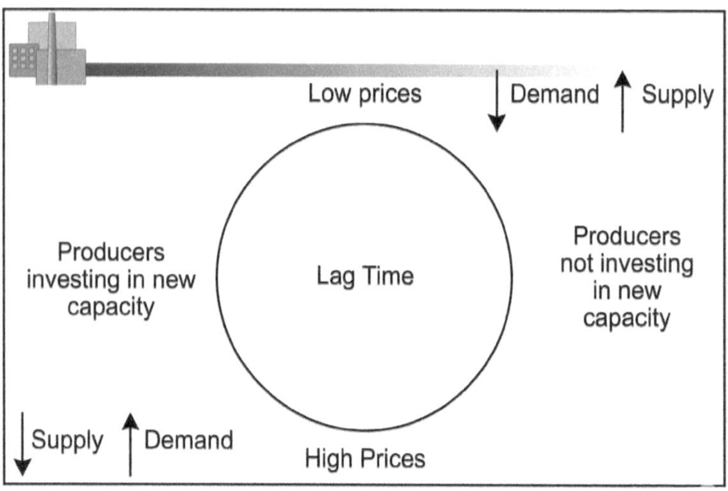

Why are Commodities Important for Investors?

Commodities do well when the other asset classes are under pressure. For example, these might perform when stocks are under pressure. The rationale is commonsensical - as commodities increase in price, cost of raw materials for companies rises. This results in lower corporate earnings, thus impacting stock prices.

Moreover, higher commodity prices will cause inflation to increase, which in turn results in higher interest rates. This will have a further detrimental effect on stock prices because of higher borrowing costs for companies. Long-term bonds also deliver poor investment returns in inflationary conditions.

Commodities, therefore, become a good source of diversification and reduce portfolio risk. Data from several countries also shows commodities to be a better hedge against inflation compared to stocks and bonds.

Returns-wise also, the performance of commodities is impressive. In their bull cycle, they are capable of delivering stock-like high returns. Overall, commodities are a beneficial addition to the portfolio

Risks - Why are Commodities Reserves rather than Main Players

We saw in Chapter 8 that long-term charts from various countries demonstrate that stock values are always upward sloping, in spite of lots of unpredictability and volatility in the short-term. The reason is simple: stock prices reflect economic growth. Stocks, therefore, deliver consistent returns on a long-term basis.

Contrastingly, long-term studies do not show commodities producing great consistent returns. For example, Jeremy Siegel's research (graph shown in Chapter 8) shows that 1 U.S. dollar invested in stocks in 1802 would have become 8.80 million U.S. dollars in the year 2001, while the same dollar invested in gold would have remained at merely 14.38 dollars.

The reason is simple - commodities have a self-limiting price mechanism. No commodity will keep showing a price that just keeps on increasing. On the other hand, its price will move in a range. This is because of demand and supply reacting vigorously to extremes of prices.

For example, if sugar becomes very expensive, pecuniary considerations might modify the salivation reflexes of people with a sweet tooth. On the other side of the equation, higher prices will affect the reflexes of sugar suppliers in the opposite way. Lag time, as described in the commodity business cycle, might keep the price high for some time. But that is bound to fall in the future.

Sugar price history is illustrative. It was at 1.5 cents per pound in 1966. Then it spurted to reach 66 cents in 1974. In 1976 it was down to 8 cents and in 1985 to 2.5 cents. After a long time, in 2005-06, it is again rising, but perhaps the next peak might still remain lower than the peak of 1974.

Therefore, there is no doubt that in the bull phase, commodities can produce astonishingly high returns. Moreover, the bull run can last for a long time too. But because of the pronounced cycle, prices fall rapidly.

Consequently, while stocks become almost a default asset class of each portfolio, commodities are useful when their demand-supply is in a certain configuration; and it is important for investors to take that into consideration. The following simple valuation questions will facilitate decision-making.

Valuation of Commodities

Every commodity will have its own demand-supply curve that is not synchronized with other commodities. For each commodity, in order to determine whether the commodity is under or overvalued, investors should seek answers to the following questions from the commodity fund advisor/manager:

Demand

- What is the commodity utilized for? What is the present demand and its growth?
- What is the state of the economic cycle and relation to commodity usage?
- Which of its functions will be valid in the future? Impact of new developments?
- Can the commodity be replaced by cheaper or better alternatives?

Supply

- What are the existing inventories and their relation to current and expected demand?
- What are the sources of supply and their efficiency?
- What are the locations of sources and their vulnerability, if any?
- Is there a lag time in increasing supplies over the next few years?
- Are there new sources of supply and what are the cost-benefit dynamics?

How to Invest in Commodities?

There can be several ways to invest in commodities, namely:

- Commodity futures on exchanges
- Mutual funds in commodities
- Index funds linked to commodity indices

- Investing in companies dealing in commodities
- Investing in countries rich in commodities

Commodity Markets in India

India is rapidly becoming a very important market for commodities. There are three national online multiple commodity exchanges and twenty-two commodity specific exchanges. For example, National Commodity & Derivatives Exchange of India (NCDEX) currently offers trading in 48 commodities. Daily average volume is expanding rapidly and is expected to show significant growth in the coming years.

Banks, Mutual Funds and FIIs will soon be involved in the commodities markets. Commodity funds are also likely to be launched in the near future. Gold ETF (exchange traded fund) is also on the anvil. Investors can buy and sell units with gold as the underlying asset for as little as Rs.100. Units can be traded in the same manner as units of Mutual Funds.

Art

Definition

Art is the application of skill to the production of visible beauty and works of creative imagination. It is an expression common to all cultures, though the representation and articulation might reflect the diversity.

Business Cycle & Art

Art, too, has a linkage to the general business cycle. In a growing economy, more wealth gets created and demand for Art increases. Therefore, prices appreciate. However, since art is essentially owned by ultra-high-net-worth individuals, they might hang onto it irrespective of a downturn in business cycle. Therefore, one can say that art is fairly immune to business cycle downturns, while good times cause a higher appreciation, not only of the work but also of the price.

Classification

One of the common ways of classifying art is based on the period in which a particular work was created:

- Old Masters (1300 – 1860)
- Impressionists (1860 – 1920)
- Modern (1920 – 1970)
- Contemporary (1970 – 1985)
- Very contemporary (1985 onwards)

Why Art

Art qualifies as a reserve player in the portfolio because:

- It is a scarce product, not reproducible at will
- It combines aesthetics with investment
- It has an ever-increasing demand coupled with an absolutely limited supply
- It has low correlation with other financial assets
- It has the ability to survive an economic downturn
- Long-term trend for art prices is up

Returns

The Mei Moses All Art Index, based on resale values of paintings sold at public auction in New York, has become a good measurement indicator of art value since 1875. The Index has outperformed fixed income but underperformed equity from 1875 to 2000. However, from 2000 to 2003, it has outperformed equities also.

Risks - Why is Art a Reserve and not a Main Player?

Art is at best an alternative investment product because:

- Its authenticity and quality are difficult to judge
- It has low transparency
- It requires very long-term investment horizon
- Art is illiquid
- It has high transaction and storage costs
- It has no intrinsic value
- Auction fraud may be involved
- Accounting standardization is absent
- Regulation and recourse for investors is minimal

Indian Art Paints a Global Picture

During the last few years, Indian Art has made a much deeper impression globally. More and more galleries are displaying Indian art all over the world; and there are increasing numbers of buyers entering Indian art auctions. The number of paintings and artists

Lester Anthony Paul

Lester Anthony Paul

being sold has risen and the prices have jumped 6-8 times. Some recent examples are:

- 'Mystic repast' by Francis Newton Souza for $153,000 at Sotheby's in New York
- 'Celebration' by Tyeb Mehta for $317,500 at Christie's in New York
- M.F. Husain's work for $435,000 as a private sale

Indian art is still highly undervalued, with an average price of $50,000 compared to $400,000 of a comparable Chinese or Indonesian painting. It is becoming a key sideshow to the evolution of India as an economic super power.

Trends in Art Investing

- Art advisory firms
- Private equity funds
- Financial institutions building up large databases for various segments of the art market
- Art banking – banks utilizing art experts to build art portfolios for wealthy clients

Developments in the Indian Art market

Art Index

Economic Times has unveiled the ET Art Index, which could become a useful benchmark for fund managers and art investors. To launch this index, data on transactions of artworks belonging to 51 leading contemporary artists has been utilized. The transaction value of these 51 artists comprises 88% of the total organized

Indian art market in the year 2005. Some of the artists included in the index are Jamini Roy, A.R. Chughtai, M.F. Husain, Souza, Tyeb Mehta, Gaitonde, Ganesh Pyne, Bhupen Khakhar and the three Tagores.

This index is calculated on the basis of the average square inch rate (SIR) of works of art of these top artists. This is calculated by dividing the sale value by the area/volume of the artwork.

The index took a base value of 100 on January 1, 1998 and stood at 2513.1 on March 22, 2006. On a compounded annualized basis, the ET art index gave a very impressive return of 47.8% since its inception.

Art Funds

Art funds are also being launched that enable investors to invest in art even if they do not understand it. The mechanism is like that of a fund in any other asset class. Characteristics of a recently launched fund are:

- Art expert designated as fund manager
- Fund manager responsible for buying and selling works of art
- Minimum amount of investment (Rs.10 lakh in this fund) from each investor
- Close-ended fund

It is possible that in about 2-3 years' time, a structure might be created for an art mutual fund with units of much smaller denomination and under the purview of a regulator.

Conclusion

Alternative asset classes are useful adjuncts to portfolios. They many times perform well when the traditional asset classes are under pressure. They have a history of generating high stock-like returns and therefore can perform a very beneficial task of increasing portfolio returns while reducing risk by providing diversification.

However, the same principles of investing are applicable to these classes as well. Investor should be fully aware of the unique characteristics and risks of each asset class. Due diligence is equally required in terms of valuation.

Finally, it is important to note that while these assets should be developed as reserve players, investors should not rely on them as main players.

Part 4

Special Factors

Courtesy: Pradeep Mandhani/imageallsports.com

Umpire Billy Bowden - Rules & regulations important determinants of a player's performance

Chapter 16

Investment Taxation - Regulation Influencing Team Selection

Introduction

Rahul is contemplating technicalities of the game – the myriad rules and regulations which have often changed the shape of a game........ field restrictions during the first 10 overs and two subsequent power plays, bowlers being allowed a maximum of 10 overs, what constitutes a legal bowling action, and when a ball is adjudged wide. Rahul considers the importance of these rules and realizes that understanding the various mechanics, procedures and conventions is as essential as basic play. Certain regulations might favour a particular player's style while being detrimental to another's natural style, and therefore, team selection should look at this aspect too. Adapting quickly to important rules can make the difference between victory and defeat.

Moreover, rules and regulations are not static; they have their own dynamism. For example, the role of technology is assuming greater importance. Any line decision can be referred to the third umpire who has the benefit of replays to judge whether a batsman is out or not. Gradually, that role is expanding to other decisions as well. It is important to keep abreast of the latest developments.

Similarly, regulations governing financial markets are also dynamic and constantly evolve to reflect new products and developments. One of the most important regulations is taxation, since for an investor it is essentially post taxation returns that matter. If a taxation rule is enacted which favors a particular asset class, then it becomes advantageous to have a heavier allocation to that class. For example, for a long time, small savings schemes enjoyed tax breaks that were not applicable to other asset classes. Lately, stocks have enjoyed a favorable taxation treatment with dividends being tax-free and long-term capital gains also being exempt from taxation. It is only natural that proportion of Indian savings into stocks is increasing.

Another important factor is that by enacting certain rules, the government might be trying to channelize savings in a particular direction. Then, if demand for a marketable security class gets a fillip, it goes up, thus causing even more demand. Therefore, understanding regulation is not only important for calculating your post tax returns but also for knowing where to invest, where investible money will find its way.

Furthermore, asset selection in the future will be from a wider pool. Gradually, regulation in India is moving to approve commodities funds and real estate funds. Additionally, as the process of capital convertibility goes forward, it will be possible to increase allocation to foreign investment products.

November 5. 1987, Wankhede Stadium, India vs. England, World Cup Semi-Final

It was 4th November 1987 and the England team was having a very animated meeting. It was the 4th World Cup, the first being held outside England. For the first three tournaments, in spite of being the host team, England had not been able to raise the cup. Paradoxically, they saw their best chance ever in the different conditions prevailing in the subcontinent.

However, tomorrow was the acid test. They were meeting a very motivated team and that too, in their home conditions in Mumbai. Besides, India were the defending champions having won the 1983 World Cup. So far India had done well in the competition and had reached the semi-final convincingly.

While watching the tapes of previous India matches, one thing that stood out was the dominance of two Indian spinners, Ravi Shastri and Maninder Singh. They were proving to be quite a handful on the turning tracks of India. Both were very economical and at the same time taking wickets. Against Australia at Delhi, their combined 20 overs yielded only 69 runs. Both being leg spinners, they would pitch the ball outside the leg stump and turn it in, making run scoring very difficult.

It was important to think of a way to neutralize them. A good total was very important to counteract the strong batting lineup of Gavaskar, Srikkanth, Vengsarkar, Sidhu, Azharuddin supported by all-rounders Kapil and Shastri.

The mood in the meeting was turning sombre when Gooch startled everybody by saying 'I will literally sweep them off their own ground'. When asked to elaborate, he said that he intends taking full advantage of the rule that a batsman cannot be given out LBW if the ball pitches outside leg stump.

Next morning, there was a lot of excitement and an air of expectancy in India. Wankhede Stadium was packed to capacity. India won the toss, put England in to bat and strode out confidently. As in the previous matches they brought on their spinners quickly and Maninder Singh responded by getting Robinson out. Athey also did not last long and that brought in Gatting and Gooch together. Gooch now started implementing his plan to the hilt. He just would not leave any ball pitched outside the leg stump. He would go down on his knees and sweep it to the fine leg or square leg area.

He went on to score 115 and with Gatting supporting him well they had a good total of 254 for 6 in their 50 overs. The two leg spinners gave away 103 runs between them in their 20 overs. Gooch's sweeping had given them the extra 30-35 runs which proved to be decisive.

In 1987, chasing 254 was a difficult target and once India lost Gavaskar early on, England's bowlers kept the pressure on. Indian batsmen were getting out at regular intervals. In spite of Azharuddin scoring 64 and Kapil's brisk 30 in 22 balls, the Indian innings folded up for 219 runs, thus losing the match by 35 runs.

Man of the match was unanimously and obviously Graham Gooch, who had utilized an important game rule to the team's advantage and won such an important match for his team.

Investment Taxation

Investments are evaluated from a risk and return perspective. However, their returns could be altered in a significant way by taxation treatment. There is a lot of clutter and redundant detail in taxation information on various investment instruments. An effective, simple, and concise way is to examine taxation of any instrument at three levels to gauge the post-taxation return-

1. Contribution: just by investing in certain instruments, the tax paid in a particular year can be reduced.

2. Earnings: Earnings can come in various forms like interest income, rental income, dividends and capital gains. Some earnings are totally exempt, while some attract taxation at different rates.

3. Maturity Amount: taxation treatment of maturity amount also varies from instrument to instrument. On redemption of any investment, the maturity amount is a combination of principal and earnings. Since taxation on earnings is being dealt with separately, essentially, this section deals with taxation treatment of principal amount when the asset is sold.

Combined taxation at all three levels or exemption at one or more levels changes the return dimension of a particular asset class significantly.

1. Equity Funds

Contributions

Contributions to a specific class of funds known as Equity Linked Saving Schemes (ELSS) are eligible under Section 80C. These reduce taxable income by a maximum of Rs. 100,000 in one year. Investing in other stock funds does not qualify for this exemption. ELSS, unlike other stock funds, has a lock-in period of 3 years.

Earnings

Earnings from stock funds come either in the form of dividends or capital gains. Dividends have a taxation rate of zero. Short-term capital gains (units held for less than 1 year) are taxed at 10% while long-term capital gains (units held for more than 1 year) have zero taxation.

Maturity Amount

Principal amount on redemption does not attract any taxation. This is applicable even to ELSS, although it saved tax on the principal amount at the time of investment.

2. Direct Equity

Taxation treatment is completely similar to equity mutual funds. Contributions to certain specified stock issues reduce taxable income under Section 80 C. Securities Transaction Tax is applicable for both Stock Funds and direct equity transactions.

3. Debt Mutual Funds

Contributions

These are not eligible for any tax deduction.

Earnings

Earnings are in the form of dividends and capital gains with the distinction between short-term and long-term gains being based on the duration of one year. Dividends are free from taxation in the hands of the investor. However, a Mutual Fund Company pays a dividend distribution tax of 12.5%, which affects the fund's NAV and therefore the investor is indirectly paying this tax. Short-term capital gains are taxed at the investor's marginal taxation rate while long-term capital gain at 10%.

Maturity Amount

Principal amount is not counted as part of taxable income on redemption of investment.

4. Small Saving Schemes

These comprise multiple schemes with distinctive characteristics and taxation treatment. They are described in Chapter 11.

5. Real Estate

Contributions

There are housing loan related tax advantages. Repayment of principal amount of housing loan qualifies again under section 80C for reducing taxable income with an upper limit of Rs.100,000 in one year. Additionally, interest on housing loan reduces taxable income by a further Rs.150,000.

Earnings

Earnings are in the form of rentals or capital gain.

- Rentals add to the total taxable income and therefore get taxed at the marginal rate.
- Capital gains result when a house is sold. Definition of short-term and long-term is different from stocks, with the relevant time period being three years compared to one year. Short-term gains are taxed at the marginal rate. Long-term capital gains are taxed at 20%, with the advantage of cost indexation. Cost of acquisition is indexed utilizing Cost Inflation Index as notified by the government.
- Long-term capital gain is exempt from tax if the seller of the property utilizes this gain to purchase or construct another residential house. This fresh property purchase has to be within a period of one year before or two years after the sale. He gets three years if he is constructing fresh property.

- Another way to save tax on long-term capital gains is to invest these gains in Capital Gains Bonds. These bonds are issued by specified institutions like Rural Electrification Corporation (REC), and tax benefits are available under Section 54EC of the Income Tax Act. Bonds have to be bought within a period of six months from the date of transfer of property. These are redeemable after 36 months and their interest income is taxable.

Maturity Amount

Principal amount on redemption is not part of taxable income.

6. Insurance products

Contributions

These also qualify under section 80C with an upper limit of Rs. 100,000.

Earnings

Earnings on the sum invested are free from taxation.

Maturity Amount

Total maturity amount is free from taxation.

7. Pension products

Contributions

These also qualify under section 80C with an upper limit of Rs. 100,000

Earnings

Earnings on the sum invested are free from taxation

Maturity Amount

On maturity, 2/3 of the total amount has to be utilized to buy an annuity. Periodic annuity payments are subject to taxation. However, 1/3 amount received as a lump sum is free from any taxation

Conclusion

For any investor, what matters is the post-taxation return. Therefore, investment taxation rules can make a tremendous difference to the relative attractiveness of various asset classes.

The easiest and most effective way to analyze taxation of any instrument is to look at the treatment at three levels:

1. Whether investing in an asset reduces tax liability?

2. What are the earnings of the asset class and how are those taxed?

3. What happens when the asset matures or is sold?

Indian taxation rules have lately become a lot more favourable for stocks. On the other hand, small savings schemes have suffered relatively. These had exclusive advantages earlier; but now, with no sectoral caps in Section 80 C, they have had to compete with other asset classes.

Government also utilizes taxation incentives to channel savings in certain classes; therefore, regulation could be useful in forecasting where savings are going to be invested. Consequently, it is one of the indicators facilitating a view on future returns of an asset class.

Rahul realizes he should also take this aspect into account while picking his team. Overall, a clear and concise understanding of taxation could make a lot of difference in whether one wins or loses the wealth game.

Courtesy: Pradeep Mandhani/imageallsports.com

Capitalizing on Indian opportunity
Nasser Hussain, ex England captain of Indian origin,
expert commentator in the recent India - Pakistan series

Chapter 17

NRI Opportunity - India as an Attractive Investment Destination

India - One of the most important cricketing nations in the 21st Century

Rahul finds the history of the game very interesting. It was in the 8th century when two shepherds in Northern Europe thought of a diversion from grazing their sheep. One picked up a stick, while the other a stone. The stick shepherd stood in front of a wicket gate in a paddock fence and had to hit the stone as far as possible and that was the beginning of this immensely popular game.

The Normans brought the game to England during the conquest of the Saxons in 1066. In England, the game really developed with standardization of pitch length, wicket height and width, weight and shape of ball and bat as well as evolution of various rules. Then in 1864 over-arm bowling was allowed, which revolutionized the game by making the contest between bat and ball equal.

On March 15, 1877, the first test match was played in Melbourne between Australia and England, and Australia won by 45 runs. Cricket has also been played in the Olympics, though only once - in the year 1900 in Paris. France expectedly won the silver medal.

Only two teams were participating, and Great Britain won the gold.

For a number of years, England and Australia dominated the running of the game. On 15th June 1909, the Imperial Cricket Conference (ICC) was formed with just 3 members – England, Australia and South Africa. ICC is now known as International Cricket Council and all Test playing countries enjoy equal standing. In August 2005, ICC left its base at Lord's to set up its new headquarters in Dubai.

Who would have thought that in the year 2006, India would be the most important cricketing nation in the world? The nation with the wealthiest cricket control board, the most passionate cricket fans and companies that believed that people would stop shaving if their cricket icon did not endorse a shaving cream. The game had turned a full circle. It was indeed a proud moment when Iqbal, a direct descendant of the stone-throwing, sheep-grazing shepherd of the 8th century, turned up appropriately in Indian colours as a top quality fast bowler.

India - One of the Most Important Economies in 21st century

If the world cricket order could turn around so dramatically, so could the world economic order. Goldman Sachs, one of the most prestigious investment banks in the USA, in its widely quoted BRIC (Brazil, Russia, India & China) report in 2003, forecast that the world will be a radically different place in 2050. China will be the largest economy followed by the USA, India, Japan, Brazil, and Russia in that order. Only two of the current top six economies (USA and Japan) figure on their list.

The report also predicts major currency appreciation in BRIC countries. As per capita income rises, currency converges towards its purchasing power parity (PPP) rate. By that estimate, in 2050, a U.S. dollar may have less than 20 Indian Rupees.

These conclusions are not as surprising as they appear at first look, the report argues. In 1960, Japan was a low-income nation, and in the next 30 years went on to become the second largest economy. Japanese yen appreciated 300% against US dollar in that period. Korea grew at a tremendous rate between 1970 and 2000. China within the last 10 years has managed to make a great impact.

Besides, their conclusions are based on valid modeling techniques, assumptions that take into account employment generation, capital stock formation, and purchasing power parity. Their model, if applied in 1960, would have predicted Japan's growth quite correctly. They would have predicted that Russia would grow much faster than what actually happened, but Russia's economic growth was stymied by political upheaval.

The past few years have seen India developing as predicted. Economic growth rate has been in the range of 7-8%; inflation has been well controlled; the central bank has a very prudent policy; reforms are on track; political stability is there; the currency has appreciated slightly against the US dollar; corporate earnings are growing at a healthy clip, and the fiscal deficit is declining.

Sustainability of Fast GDP Growth in India

India has a very young population and on a relative basis, stands out even more since Europe and Japan are ageing speedily. Indian demographics are a decisive factor in terms of not only the proportion of young people, but English-speaking abilities and proficiency in information technology skills. The twin factors of technology and globalization make outsourcing an important development, beneficial for India with its major cost advantage. Additionally, Indian domestic market is large; and hence, the economy is consumption-led and not export dependent.

Rahul considers the various components of GDP. It is the sum of consumption, investment, government spending, and surplus of exports over imports. Consumption is increasing at a good clip with effective employment generation. There is a big growing middle class with rising consumer aspirations. Consumer credit is also growing with considerable potential to grow further, since it is still at a much lower level compared to similar economies.

Capital investment is also increasing rapidly, as capacity utilization in various industries has risen to 85-90%. Government is also adding to economic growth by investing substantial sums in infrastructure and industrial development. They are also trying to make this growth inclusive by earmarking substantial outlay for agriculture, rural development schemes, health care, and education. Export growth is also very healthy, primarily in the areas of information technology, information technology-enabled services and business process outsourcing. Even manufacturing exports are picking up.

Consequently, Indian GDP growth is expected to grow rapidly for a number of years.

NRI Investment Opportunity in India - A Compelling Proposition

Indian stock funds returned a remarkable 62% on an annualized, compounded basis in the years 2002-2005. Comparative returns in the USA were 2.7%. For Europe the figure was 13.8%, and for Latin America 52.7%.

Similarly, real estate returns in India during the same period have been much higher than returns in developed economies. With a rapidly growing economy in a densely populated, big country, the demand for residential and commercial complexes is unprecedented. The manufacturing and information technology related facilities, malls, multiplexes have led to a construction boom. Alignment of interest rates with lower global rates has led to an insatiable appetite for home loans and fueled the desire for home ownership. Supply is not keeping pace with this explosive demand and real estate prices have shot up tremendously.

Interest rates are also gradually creeping up. 10-year Indian Government Bond is yielding almost 3% more than 10-year U.S. Treasury Bond. Consequently, Indian debt funds are generating a significantly higher return.

Moreover, if we combine attractive returns with expectation of appreciation of the Indian Rupee, it becomes a compelling proposition for NRIs to invest in India. To meet financial goals, as we saw in Chapter 4, a good real rate of return on investments can make a tremendous difference. Weight of BRICs in investment portfolio has to be increasingly aligned with their potential. Some of the best-known and influential voices in global capital markets are advocating a 40% allocation to emerging markets.

Sustainability of Attractive Investment Returns in India

The tempo of fast economic growth, stellar corporate performance, movement of domestic savings towards stocks and increased allocation to emerging markets, especially India, will continue to ensure substantial returns for Indian investments.

The Indian economy is one of the fastest growing economies in the world. Leading Indian companies are spreading and growing their earnings at a healthy rate. Indian government has made stocks even more attractive by enacting very favorable taxation rules. More domestic savings are being channeled into stocks. Presently, only 3% goes into stocks compared to 45% in the USA, thus implying huge further potential.

Principles of investing in stocks and real estate, as described in chapters 8 and 9, remain the same, irrespective of their geographic location. One has to take into consideration appropriate time horizon, attractive valuation, and proper diversification.

Indian markets have shown volatility. For example, the huge returns of 2002-2005 were followed by a steep and speedy correction. Markets everywhere sometimes move ahead of economic growth and sometimes lag behind, but retain their propensity to revert to the mean. So, a correction in a fundamentally strong market provides another opportunity to enter, by making valuations attractive.

Overall, with the Indian economy moving inexorably towards its rightful place in the global order, the Non-Resident Indians has a tremendous opportunity to participate in this growth story by investing a part of their portfolios in India, especially when NRIs can invest so easily in India as far as regulations and transaction mechanics are concerned.

Who is a Non-Resident Indian (NRI)

As the name suggests there are two parts to the term Non-Resident Indian:

Non-Resident: There are different definitions and exceptions under FEMA (Foreign Exchange Management Act, 1999) and Income Tax Act, 1961. However, the simplest definition that covers most scenarios is that if somebody has stayed for less than 182 days in India in the preceding financial year, he is a non-resident.

Indian: this includes Indian citizen or Person of Indian Origin (PIO), where PIO is defined as a citizen of any other country (other than Bangladesh or Pakistan) provided he or either of his parents or any of his grandparents was a citizen of India.

Facilities for Non-Resident Indians

NRIs can access Indian opportunities in diverse ways and investments are permitted both on repatriation and non-repatriation basis. The facilities include the following:

1. Direct investment in trade and industry
2. Establishing a branch, office or other place of business in India
3. Opening and maintaining Bank Accounts
4. Investing in immovable properties
5. Investing in shares, mutual funds, debentures, new issues and a variety of other instruments

NRI Concerns on Investing in India

Repatriation

India is moving towards full capital convertibility and has made repatriation rules, especially for NRIs, very liberal.

NRIs can open broadly two types of accounts in India. First is where the credits are from foreign exchange sources. These include NRE (non-resident external) and FCNR (foreign currency non-external) accounts. Second is NRO (non-resident ordinary) that can receive funds in Indian rupees accruing from local bona fide transactions.

Money in NRE/FCNR accounts is fully repatriable. Additionally, redemption proceeds from investments made with foreign exchange, for example, from an NRE account, are fully repatriable. However, even from an NRO account, up to a million USD can be repatriated in a calendar year.

For example, the sale proceeds of immovable property acquired using local rupee funds can be repatriated easily. The proceeds will be credited to an NRO account and, as stated above, up to USD 1 million can be repatriated in a calendar year. In its November 2006 directive, the RBI also removed the restriction of a 10-year holding period for property

Depreciation of Indian Rupee

Just a few years ago, the Indian Rupee used to very predictably depreciate against USD by a few percentage points every year. However, things have changed since 2003. After almost touching Rs.50 to a U.S. Dollar, it has since appreciated significantly, albeit with multiple corrections. With the forecasted economic growth differential, INR is expected to appreciate considerably over the years.

Taxation

Indian taxation is very favourable. For example, for stocks as described in the chapter on taxation, dividends and long-term capital gains (stocks held for more than one year) are both not taxed, while short-term capital gains tax is 10%. NRIs and residents mainly have tax parity, except for NRIs, the procedure is even simpler with no mandatory PAN (permanent account number) requirement.

Additionally, India has a double taxation avoidance agreement with numerous countries including USA, UK, UAE, Oman, Qatar, Australia, Canada, and Singapore.

Political Stability

In May 2004, after the surprising election results, markets reacted violently. However, even a seemingly unusual coalition has provided political stability which augurs well for the future. Additionally, the economic reforms process now has its own momentum and is expected to continue, irrespective of the ruling political combination.

Market Scams

Securities and Exchange Board of India (SEBI) is a lot more alert as a market regulator. Exchange systems are totally computerized and there are rigorous risk management and surveillance procedures. Multiple big players provide more depth to the market. Indian markets are safer with much lower probability of market scams and collusion.

Implementation, Execution and Monitoring

The wealth management industry is becoming more professional rapidly. Banks, both foreign and local, have started offering these services. Specialized wealth management companies and boutiques are growing in number. Wealth management training is becoming better and more accessible. It is easy for NRIs to find a professional, able and ethical partner for managing their wealth in India.

Conclusion

India is one of the fastest growing economies in the world and is expected to continue at a fast clip for quite some time. It is a big populous country rising from a low base with immense potential. The fast growth, impressive corporate performance, channeling of domestic savings into stocks, housing boom and rising attention from foreign investors are resulting in remarkable returns from its asset markets. The bull market though accompanied by corrections is likely to continue for quite some time. Moreover, Indian Rupee is also likely to appreciate over the long run.

With very easy and liberal rules and regulations for NRIs combined with well-developed and regulated capital markets, India offers a very compelling opportunity. Various concerns that affected NRI returns in the past are today, either irrelevant or much less pronounced. Overall, India is one of the most attractive investment destinations worldwide for NRIs.

Part 5

Winning the Wealth Game

Courtesy: PTI

Finally all that planning and implementation pays off

Chapter 18

Winning the Wealth Game

Introduction

The Day of Reckoning

Today is the day when everything comes together, when all his previous efforts will bear fruit. It is a nice, sunny day with a good breeze. Rahul is walking out for the toss and is taking confident steps to the middle of the packed stadium.

With each stride, he looks back at the path he has traversed after being appointed captain. He recalls the action steps he has taken and the changes he has affected......

Conviction that We Could Win

When he took over, the team was in disarray. They did not have the conviction that they could win. Rahul instilled in them a strong belief that everyone can win this game. After all, a person is wealthy if his passive income is sufficient to sustain a desirable lifestyle. It is the word desirable that makes the process so individualized.

Different people have different yardsticks and can be wealthy in their own right.

Sizing Up the Opponent and Determining Financial Goals

The team had vague and non-specific ideas about what the opponents were doing. Rahul's wealth creation team was pitted against the financial needs team. He ensured that the opponent was sized up well. He helped in prioritizing, identifying, and quantifying the financial goals. It has been proven that probability of winning goes up significantly if goals are well defined.

Organizing Information

Rahul was stunned and absolutely disbelieving that all their financial information was so disorganized. Even simple questions like how much of the assets are allocated to stocks were going unanswered. There was no distinction between real estate for own usage and real estate for investment. He responded by organizing and marshalling all the scattered bits of important information. He utilized a one-page scorecard that tells him the current situation and the progress the team is making at one glance.

Taking a Macro perspective - Determining Strategy

Rahul was totally bewildered that there was no strategy in place. There was no thought to the state of the pitch - whether it was conducive to stroke play or to a more defensive strategy. There was no thought given to business cycle staging. He realized the importance of reading the pitch well to determine whether it is conducive to good stroke play enabling a good total or it is imperative to employ a defensive strategy. He is happy but mystified that for such a beneficial aspect the process is disproportionately easy and quick.

Similarly personal life cycle factors were not given any consideration. After all, a young person will have a different allocation compared to a retired person since the needs are so different.

Cultivating a Winning Mindset

Rahul was aghast to see such low team morale. After all, who does not work under uncertainty and volatile circumstances - isn't this an integral part of life? That does not mean that opportunity does not exist. Cultivating a winning mindset improved investment results significantly.

Selecting an Effective Team

Rahul was initially perplexed when he saw that he had been given a strange team. However, his surprise was short-lived. If there is no strategic perspective, team selection too, cannot be appropriate. Moreover, zonal biases and horse-trading were rampant. The previous coach had termed selection meetings a big farce. For example, there was too much reliance on small savings that are clearly over the hill. Additionally, insurance, which is necessary but only as a 12th man on current performance was being given top billing. Dirty politics had branded a consistent performer like Stocks as a very risky batsman and dented his confidence.

Rahul overcame all those selection biases. He was focused on winning and selected the best team possible given the business cycle and personal cycle constraints. He knows that he has to score runs while taking minimal risks. Stocks are his top strikers and an integral part of the team. These will be augmented by versatile, multifaceted real estate. The economic cycle is bound to have sticky periods and Debt will prove to be a good defensive batsman.

Small saving schemes are steadily going out of favor but in certain situations could be recalled. For example, senior citizens' saving scheme offers a good return. Insurance is absolutely important but still should be a 12th man. Taking pure protection products is mandatory but their investment returns and high costs still do not warrant a place in the team. Then the underlying winning theme is provided by a sheet anchor who keeps working towards the final victory.

Overall, he now has a much better understanding of strengths and weaknesses of various players and has selected the best possible team for prevalent conditions.

Receptive to New Talent and Developing Bench Strength

When he took over, there was no attention to developing new talent and bench strength. New products in the form of capital-guaranteed products or variable retirement annuities evoked very little interest. Some of the structured products can indeed be genuine all-rounders.

Additionally, reserve players have to be called upon when circumstances render main players ineffective. Understanding reserve players like commodities and art has made Rahul's team effective under most circumstances.

Analyzing Special Factors

Regulation can make a lot of difference between victory and defeat. Rahul was bemused and befogged that there was very little attention paid to these important aspects by the erstwhile regime.

Taxation, for example, is a very important factor; it is the post-taxation return that is meaningful. Therefore, team selection or asset allocation is heavily dependent on taxation rules. For example, a favorable taxation of stocks channeled plenty of domestic savings to stocks. Another instance is special treatment for NRI investments, like making it easier for them by not requiring a PAN number or a rationalization of TDS (tax deducted at source), which facilitated additional investment in India from NRIs. Announcement of an attractive matching pension scheme with tax benefits to boot will increase its appeal. Rahul is far more abreast of the factors that have a major effect on how assets are allocated.

July 13, 2002, Lord's Cricket Ground, India vs. England, Natwest Trophy Final

Rahul now has the last few minutes with his team before the match starts. He has a good command over strategic aspects and has selected the best possible team suited for the conditions prevalent today. However, implementation is the key and the team has to deliver on its potential.

To motivate his team, Rahul recalls one of the most exciting matches in Indian cricket history. The team executed the important doctrines to perfection mentioned above and India posted a memorable victory. Lord's, the most prestigious cricketing venue in the world, was just the right stage for such an important final match.

England won the toss and elected to bat. They got off to an electrifying start and were at one stage 227 for one in 36.5 overs. Marcus Trescothick scored 109 runs while Nasser Hussain scored 115. They accelerated even more in the final overs with Andrew Flintoff scoring a quick-fire 40 and finished with an imposing total of 325 for 5 in 50 overs.

The Indian team had really chosen an extravagant lifestyle - they had given away lots of runs. Financial needs were really challenging them. Required run rate was an imposing 6.5 runs per over. However, the team was confident of sustaining such a lifestyle.

Strategically, the team think tank had read the pitch well and it was right on target in their assessment that such a score is very much possible. The pitch was very conducive to stroke play and good returns were highly probable. In other words, economic conditions were very favourable.

Additionally, team selection was appropriate for this pitch. A hefty allocation to top strikers, given the pitch was logical. The team was studded with batsmen, with even Yuvraj and Kaif batting at numbers 6 and 7. This was not a pitch where playing an extra specialist bowler would have been good. It had just the right balance. In other words, given very good economic conditions, a heavier allocation to high-return assets like stocks and real estate was warranted.

Finally, it was the implementation that was important. Runs actually had to be scored and the team had to work hard on its batting. They had to keep their equanimity in difficult conditions. Appropriate allocation to the right assets in dynamic conditions was an important determinant of success. Tactically, this translated into the following steps:

- They had to start early. Saving and investing well could not be postponed, for example to the age of 40 years to maintain such a consistently good life style. Their intentions were made clear when Sehwag scored a blistering square cut right in the first over.

- Effective and timely deployment of yield enhancing assets was important when conditions were at their most favourable. The first 15 overs, because of restrictions on the fielding team, generated high returns and had to be utilized appropriately. So aggressive batsmen Sehwag and Ganguly opened and scored at a blistering pace : 106 runs in the first 14 overs.

- Moreover, they just could not let go of any opportune time in the business cycle. Alex Tudor and Paul Collingwood were the weak links in the bowling line-up. It was decided that the batsmen would go for them, and they hit 86 runs in 12 overs combined from these 2 bowlers.

- Each business cycle has some difficult periods but the important thing is not to be deterred. Instead, remaining focused on good fundamentals was important. India lost 5 wickets quickly including those of Tendulkar, and was 146 for 5 in 24 overs. It was like a severe stock market correction akin to Sensex dropping to 9000 from 12600 in May 2006. However, the team maintained a winning mindset. Fundamentals of easy pitch and easy bowling were still intact and the target was still very much achievable.

- Significance of appropriate team selection became evident here. Yuvraj and Kaif were involved in a 121-run partnership in less than 18 overs. Yuvraj scored 69 runs in 63 balls. The team continued to score fast in spite of the wobble in the middle of the innings. Asset allocation remained skewed towards yield enhancing assets.

Finally, India won a dramatic victory by 2 wickets with 3 balls to spare. Kaif was man of the match with an unbeaten 87 off 75 balls. After hearing about this great win, the team was just in the right frame of mind for this all-important match now.

Asset Allocation and the Batting Square

If we go back to the scorecard in Chapter 3, the entire individual financial information can be organized into 4 squares of Income, Expenses, Assets, and Liabilities. All squares can contribute to reaching financial goals. However, they have varying degrees of effectiveness.

For example, Income can be bolstered but most individuals with their set skills would have limited upside. Expense Square can be worked on too but in many instances might be the least preferred option since it affects current lifestyle. Liabilities can be useful since certain debts with high-interest rates like credit card debt can be eliminated. But this also has a restricted efficacy.

The most potent, the most efficacious, and the most useful is the Asset Square. An individual has a very wide choice of placing his assets in a huge number of investment instruments available. These include bank deposits, stocks, real estate, debt, art, commodities, structured products, and multiple other alternatives. *The process of deciding where assets are placed and in what proportion is known as asset allocation.*

The asset square is indeed the batting square, which has to put on the runs. Asset Square constitutes an individual's portfolio that in its totality has to produce a good return over an innings. There is no point if one part of the portfolio is doing well while another is losing.

Asset allocation makes the maximum difference since various asset classes, as we have seen in the previous chapters, produce contrasting returns. Moreover, returns of the same asset class in different conditions could be widely dissimilar.

Asset allocation – an optimization equation

If the objective is to maximize returns, why not simply put everything in classes that have produced the maximum returns in the past? This is like asking a question in cricket that why not go for a six off every ball? The obvious answer is, of course, that there are risks; there are constraints.

In cricket you cannot take indiscriminate risks; the whole team can get out for a paltry total. Similarly, in the wealth game, asset allocation is an optimization equation where you have to maximize returns given constraints. These constraints are of two kinds:

1. Personal cycle constraints – a common example is a retired person will need liquidity in the form of a safe stable income stream since active income is not there. Some part of his portfolio has to be devoted to assets that produce such a stream, irrespective of the magnitude of returns.
2. Economic cycle constraints - an investor might impulsively invest most of his money in real estate since a friend has made huge returns there. However, there is room for disappointment since the present business cycle stage might be hazardous for such a decision. The friend might have invested at a much better time, but now the cycle might not be conducive for such investment.

On-Field Tools for Quick Decision-Making - Asset Allocation in a Dynamic Environment

Rahul realizes that on-field implementation poses different challenges. He needs effective tools to assess his situation and to keep fine-tuning with the changing environment. He has two very useful on field tools to take care of personal cycle and economic cycle constraints, especially since these keep on changing in a person's lifetime:

On-Field Tool 1 for Personal-Cycle Constraints

Asset allocation has a hierarchy of needs. The first imperative is to take care of liquidity. Some sum has to be in very liquid instruments so that contingency and emergency expenses can be taken care of. This is an individualized decision but will generally vary between 6 to 12 months of expenses.

Second imperative is to take care of the safety aspect. We have discussed the need for absolutely safe income stream for retired persons. Assets producing such income will come under the Safety part of the portfolio. Another example is long-term assets with totally assured returns, independent of any external conditions. A government bond held till maturity is a good example. Other examples are pension schemes and real estate for own usage. Percentage allocation devoted to safety will be dependent on risk orientation of the investor.

Figure 18.1: On Field Tool 1

	PORTFOLIO		
NEEDS	INSTRUMENTS	PERCENTAGE	RETURN
LIQUIDITY			
SAFETY			
YIELD ENHANCING			

Source: Finance Doctor

On-Field Tool 2 for Economic Cycle Constraints

Once liquidity and safety have been taken care of, the third imperative and most important decision is to allocate assets to instruments that produce high returns. Then the decision is dependent on what stage the economic cycle is presently going through. Here on-field tool 2 is beneficial.

Figure 18.2: On Field Tool 2

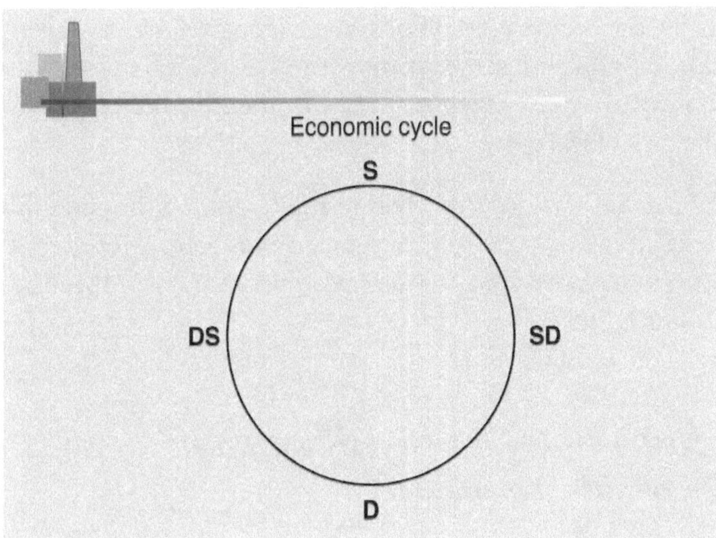

Source: Finance Doctor

The economic cycle has been described in chapters 4 and 8. Broadly summarized, it is a compass that tells us when to attack and when to defend. S stands for stocks and is the point where the team can be at its attacking best. Economic conditions are very conducive to making high returns and therefore allocation to swashbuckling stocks is highest at this point. D stands for Debt and is the point where the team has to be defensive. Economic conditions are hazardous and allocation to stocks could be hazardous. D point has the highest allocation to defensive Debt. All other points are points in between, denoting a mixed allocation to stocks and debt in varying proportions.

S point is characterized by high economic growth, low inflation, low interest rates, low P/E ratios and high corporate earnings growth rates. D point typically has low economic growth, medium to high inflation and correspondingly high interest rates, high P/E ratios and low corporate earnings growth rates.

The Match Description

Finally, the moment everybody was waiting for arrives. There is deafening applause as the opening pair walks in. All the spectators are aware of and looking forward to various undulating phases, hallmarks of this game.

The match is divided broadly into five stages and the good thing is that an investor can join the game at any stage. However, it is better to start playing as soon as possible since the probability of winning is higher.

STAGE 1- Young, 25-30 years old, Single
The Wealth Accumulator

Scenario 1

This young person has to build up and accumulate a lot of wealth. He looks at the pitch and it is very conducive to run-making. The economy is growing at a good rate, stocks are relatively undervalued, inflation is well controlled, and interest rates are at a low level. Moreover, his risk-taking capability is high. For example, initially all his wickets are intact and a lot of chances can be taken.

He adopts an aggressive approach. Top strikers are deployed with a high allocation of 80% to stocks. Safety at this stage gets only a meagre 10%. Liquidity for any contingencies will remain a constant at 10% throughout the match.

SCENARIO 1—Young, single person with good economic conditions

25-30 years old single person, wealth accumulator

P/E at 12, GDP at 8%, earnings growth at 20%, low inflation and interest rates at 5%

ASSET ALLOCATION		
Liquidity	*6–12 mths basic expense*	**allocation %**
	short term deposits	10%
	liquid funds	
	TOTAL LIQUIDITY	*10%*
Safety	*current income generating*	
	bonds with coupon	
	saving schemes with periodic income	
	real estate on rent	
	short term debt funds	
	monthly income plans	
	long term	
	provident fund	
	contributory pension schemes	10%
	small savings schemes	
	real estate for own usage	
	fixed term deposits	
	jewellery	
	TOTAL SAFETY	*10%*
Yield Enhancing		
	stocks-direct & stock funds	80%
	real estate for investment	
	bonds & bond funds	
	Pension ULIPs & others	
	commodities	
	art, antique	
	structured products	
	TOTAL YIELD ENHANCING	*80%*
TOTAL ASSETS		*100%*

SCENARIO 2—Young single person with not so favourable economic conditions

25–30 years single person, wealth accumulator

P/E at 22, GDP at 7%, earnings growth at 12%, medium inflation and interest rates at 9%

ASSET ALLOCATION		
Liquidity	*6–12 mths basic expense*	allocation %
	short term deposits	10%
	liquid funds	
	TOTAL Liquidity	*10%*
Safety	*current income generating*	
	bonds with coupon	
	saving schemes with periodic income	
	real estate on rent	
	short term debt funds	
	monthly income plans	
	long term	
	provident fund	
	contributory pension schemes	10%
	small savings schemes	
	real estate for own usage	
	fixed term deposits	
	TOTAL SAFETY	*10%*
Yield Enhancing		
	stocks-direct & stock funds	50%
	real estate for investment	
	bonds & bond funds	30%
	Pension ULIPs & others	
	commodities	
	art, antique	
	structured products	
	TOTAL YIELD ENHANCING	*80%*
TOTAL ASSETS		*100%*

Scenario 2

The team is doing well when suddenly confronted with a hostile bowler. GDP growth slows down a trifle and with it, corporate earnings. Stocks are overvalued while inflation has started picking up. The central bank starts raising interest rates.

They lose a couple of quick wickets. They now have to preserve their gains during this stage of the game. A defensive batsman is employed who might not score fast but will prevent further inroads into the innings.

Stage 2 - Relatively Young, 30-40 years old, Married, Still a Wealth Accumulator

Scenario 3

The innings enters a slightly mature phase where a sheet anchor who keeps the team focused on reaching a winning total has to be there. After a good start, risk-taking is not as much as in the beginning and some safety measures have to be adopted. At this stage allocation to contributory pension schemes and real estate for own usage increases. At the same time, looking at good economic conditions, top strikers like stocks and real estate are again put to work for accumulating as many runs as possible.

Scenario 4

The opponents are frustrated and their fast bowlers unleash bouncers. However, the batsmen are not bothered and go about their business of making runs. Bowlers are restrained and warned by the umpires.

Terrorists strike a major city but economic fundamentals are the same. The country shows lots of resilience and the stock markets actually go up upon the continuation of the same good economic fundamentals. Allocation remains exactly the same.

SCENARIO 3—*Relatively young married person with good economic conditions*

30–40 years, married, wealth accumulator
P/E at *12*, GDP at *8%*, earnings growth at *20%*, low inflation and and interest rates at *5%*

ASSET ALLOCATION		
Liquidity	*6–12 mths basic expense*	allocation %
	short term deposits	10%
	liquid funds	
	TOTAL LIQUIDITY	10%
Safety	*current income generating*	
	bonds with coupon	
	saving schemes with periodic income	
	real estate on rent	
	short term debt funds	
	monthly income plans	
	long term	
	provident fund	
	contributory pension schemes	15%
	small savings schemes	
	real estate for own usage	10%
	fixed term deposits	
	jewellery	
	TOTAL SAFETY	25%
Yield Enhancing		
	stocks-direct & stock funds	50%
	real estate for investment	15%
	bonds & bond funds	30%
	Pension ULIPs & others	
	commodities	
	art, antique	
	structured products	
	TOTAL YIELD ENHANCING	65%
TOTAL ASSETS		100%

SCENARIO 4—*Terrorist strikes in a major city- no change in allocation, remaining with fundamentals*

30-40 years, married, wealth accumulator

P/E at 12, GDP at 8%, earnings growth at 20%, low inflation and interest rates at 5%

ASSET ALLOCATION		
Liquidity	*6–12 mths basic expense*	allocation %
	short term deposits	10%
	liquid funds	
	TOTAL LIQUIDITY	*10%*
Safety	*current income generating*	
	bonds with coupon	
	saving schemes with periodic income	
	real estate on rent	
	short term debt funds	
	monthly income plans	
	long term	
	provident fund	
	contributory pension schemes	15%
	small savings schemes	
	real estate for own usage	10%
	fixed term deposits	
	TOTAL SAFETY	25%
Yield Enhancing		
	stocks-direct & stock funds	50%
	real estate for investment	15%
	bonds & bond funds	
	Pension ULIPs & others	
	commodities	
	art, antique	
	structured products	
	TOTAL YIELD ENHANCING	65%
TOTAL ASSETS		*100%*

Scenario 5

The rival captain brings back his hostile bowler. He is using him in short spells and sets up an attacking field with many fielders in catching positions. Like in Stage 1 with similar conditions, there has to be a judicious mix of attack and defense.

Again stock allocation goes down while bond allocation goes up since the cycle is near D point. The good thing is that the profits on stocks are automatically preserved when allocation moves from stocks to bonds.

Stage 3 –40-55 years old with Children Wealth Transitional Stage

Scenario 6

The innings moves to a more mature stage. There is a greater need for consolidation, while at the same time advancing the total more and more towards a winning one. In this age group of 40-55 years, some of the major financial goals like children's education has to be fulfilled. Pension schemes and real estate for own use now form a greater part of the assets. At the same time, monthly income has to be bolstered by generating a stable income stream from investments. However, economic conditions are good and therefore, stocks and real estate are deployed aggressively within the personal cycle constraints.

Protection need is higher at this stage and it might be prudent to increase the cover of term insurance. Similarly, health insurance will also have to be bolstered.

SCENARIO 5—Relatively young married person with not so favourable economic conditions

30–40 years, married, wealth accumulator
P/E at 22, GDP at 7%, earnings growth at 12%, medium inflation and interest rates at 9%

ASSET ALLOCATION		
Liquidity	*6–12 mths basic expense*	allocation %
	short term deposits	*10%*
	liquid funds	
	TOTAL LIQUIDITY	*10%*
Safety	*current income generating*	
	bonds with coupon	
	saving schemes with periodic income	
	real estate on rent	
	short term debt funds	
	monthly income plans	
	long term	
	provident fund	
	contributory pension schemes	*15%*
	small savings schemes	
	real estate for own usage	*10%*
	fixed term deposits	
	TOTAL SAFETY	*25%*
Yield Enhancing		
	stocks-direct & stock funds	*20%*
	real estate for investment	*15%*
	bonds & bond funds	*30%*
	Pension ULIPs & others	
	commodities	
	art, antique	
	structured products	
	TOTAL YIELD ENHANCING	*65%*
TOTAL ASSETS		*100%*

SCENARIO 6—Middle aged married with children, Wealth Transitional Stage

40–55 years, children's educational expense up, higher stable monthly income reqd.

P/E at 12, GDP at 8%, earnings growth at 20%,low inflation and interest rates at 5%

ASSET ALLOCATION		
Liquidity	*6–12 mths basic expense*	allocation %
	short term deposits	10%
	liquid funds	
	TOTAL LIQUIDITY	10%
Safety	*current income generating*	
	bonds with coupon	
	saving schemes with periodic income	
	real estate on rent	
	short term debt funds	
	monthly income plans	10%
	long term	
	provident fund	
	contributory pension schemes	15%
	small savings schemes	
	real estate for own usage	20%
	fixed term deposits	
	TOTAL SAFETY	45%
Yield Enhancing		
	stocks-direct & stock funds	30%
	real estate for investment	15%
	bonds & bond funds	
	Pension ULIPs & others	
	commodities	
	art, antique	
	structured products	
	TOTAL YIELD ENHANCING	45%
TOTAL ASSETS		*100%*

Scenario 7

There is an added benefit, a windfall - spouse gets a very lucrative assignment and is back in the workforce; children have reached a certain age. A bowler sent in as a pinch hitter has turned in a good batting performance. This enhanced liquidity allows the team to take additional risk. Allocation to yield-enhancing assets is correspondingly increased.

Scenario 8

Global economy is growing at a fast clip. Populous countries like China and India are showing growth rates of 8-10%. The demand for commodities is picking up and investment experts are calling for a long bull cycle.

With prosperity has come cultural consciousness. A strong India story has evoked tremendous enthusiasm for Bollywood and Indian Art.

Allocation to Art and Commodities is warranted, albeit as reserve asset classes and in a much lesser proportion than stocks and real estate.

Scenario 9

The ball is slightly old and softer. The rival captain brings on his renowned spinner who manages to secure a breakthrough. The wealth creation team again has to take a breather and play defensively for some time and tide over this difficult period.

Scenario 10

Some relief comes in the form of dropped catches from the fielding team. The government announces that stocks will qualify for tax incentives. This gives a major fillip to the asset class as more savings flow in. Consequently, more risk-taking is possible in the form of increased allocation to stocks.

SCENARIO 7—Middle aged married with children, double income high liquidity

40–55 years, spouse goes back to workforce and gets a lucrative assignment

P/E at 12, GDP at 8%, earnings growth at 20%, low inflation and interest rates at 5%

ASSET ALLOCATION		
Liquidity	*6–12 mths basic expense*	allocation %
	short term deposits	10%
	liquid funds	
	TOTAL LIQUIDITY	*10%*
Safety	*current income generating*	
	bonds with coupon	
	saving schemes with periodic income	
	real estate on rent	
	short term debt funds	
	monthly income plans	
	long term	
	provident fund	
	contributory pension schemes	15%
	small savings schemes	
	real estate for own usage	20%
	fixed term deposits	
	TOTAL SAFETY	*35%*
Yield Enhancing		
	stocks-direct & stock funds	35%
	real estate for investment	20%
	bonds & bond funds	
	Pension ULIPs & others	
	commodities	
	art, antique	
	structured products	
	TOTAL YIELD ENHANCING	55%
TOTAL ASSETS		*100%*

SCENARIO 8–Middle aged married, global economy booming, commodities demand up

40–55 years, prosperous times with enhanced culture consciousness
P/E at 12, GDP at 8%, earnings growth at 20%, low inflation and interest rates at 5%

ASSET ALLOCATION

Liquidity	*6–12 mths basic expense*	**allocation %**
	short term deposits	10%
	liquid funds	
	TOTAL LIQUIDITY	*10%*
Safety	*current income generating*	
	bonds with coupon	
	saving schemes with periodic income	
	real estate on rent	
	short term debt funds	
	monthly income plans	
	long term	
	provident fund	
	contributory pension schemes	15%
	small savings schemes	
	real estate for own usage	20%
	fixed term deposits	
	TOTAL SAFETY	35%
Yield Enhancing		
	stocks-direct & stock funds	25%
	real estate for investment	15%
	bonds & bond funds	
	Pension ULIPs & others	
	commodities	8%
	art, antique	7%
	structured products	
	TOTAL YIELD ENHANCING	55%
TOTAL ASSETS		*100%*

SCENARIO 9—*Middle aged married with not so favourable economic conditions*

40–55 years, everything else similar to scenario 6

P/E at 22, GDP at 7%, earnings growth at 12%, medium inflation and interest rates at 9%

ASSET ALLOCATION		
Liquidity	*6–12 mths basic expense*	allocation %
	short term deposits	10%
	liquid funds	
	TOTAL Liquidity	*10%*
Safety	*current income generating*	
	bonds with coupon	
	saving schemes with periodic income	
	real estate on rent	
	short term debt funds	
	monthly income plans	10%
	long term	
	provident fund	
	contributory pension schemes	15%
	small savings schemes	
	real estate for own usage	20%
	fixed term deposits	
	jewellery	
	TOTAL SAFETY	*45%*
Yield Enhancing		
	stocks-direct & stock funds	*5%*
	real estate for investment	*10%*
	bonds & bond funds	*30%*
	Pension ULIPs & others	
	commodities	
	art, antique	
	structured products	
	TOTAL YIELD ENHANCING	*45%*
TOTAL ASSETS		*100%*

SCENARIO 10—*Middle aged married, govt. announces taxation benefits for stock investment*

40–55 years , everything else similar to scenario 9, stocks get a boost
P/E at 22, GDP at 7%, earnings growth at 12%, medium inflation and interest rates at 9%

ASSET ALLOCATION		
Liquidity	*6–12 mths basic expense*	allocation %
	short term deposits	10%
	liquid funds	
	TOTAL LIQUIDITY	*10%*
Safety	*current income generating*	
	bonds with coupon	
	saving schemes with periodic income	
	real estate on rent	
	short term debt funds	5%
	monthly income plans	
	long term	
	provident fund	
	contributory pension schemes	15%
	small savings schemes	
	real estate for own usage	20%
	fixed term deposits	
	jewellery	
	TOTAL SAFETY	*40%*
Yield Enhancing		
	stocks-direct & stock funds	15%
	real estate for investment	10%
	bonds & bond funds	25%
	Pension ULIPs & others	
	commodities	
	art, antique	
	structured products	
	TOTAL YIELD ENHANCING	50%
TOTAL ASSETS		*100%*

Stage 4- 55-65 years, about to retire, Close to Wealth Harvesting Stage

Scenario 11

Here, the main objective is to take active steps to prepare for the impending loss of active income. A lot more money has to be allocated to assets that produce a safe, periodic income stream. Consequently, there is less flexibility to deploy yield enhancing assets and that allocation goes down. Interestingly, run making is never sacrificed. Even with all these personal constraints, allocation to stocks and real estate is maintained as much as possible. The team realizes that they still have a long way to go and the runs made at this juncture will come in handy at later stages.

Scenario 12

Problems arrive in clusters. If the personal constraints were not enough, the stock market showed a deep correction. This was similar to losing a couple of quick wickets of well-set batsmen. The team had a gutsy response. Economic fundamentals had not changed. On the other hand, stocks had become even more undervalued with an even lower P/E. A lusty hitter was sent in to take advantage of the situation. Allocation to stocks was augmented.

Scenario 13

All good things come to an end. The lusty hitter performed well, but as expected this was a cameo. However, it helped in adding some very valuable runs. The rival captain brought in the hostile bowler for his final spell and managed to contain the runs.

SCENARIO 11—*About to retire person, reaching wealth harvesting stage*

55–65 years old, to generate even, stable income replacing active income
P/E at 12, GDP at 8%, earnings growth at 20%, low inflation and interest rates at 5%

ASSET ALLOCATION		
Liquidity	*6–12 mths basic expense*	allocation %
	short term deposits	10%
	liquid funds	
	TOTAL LIQUIDITY	*10%*
Safety	*current income generating*	
	bonds with coupon	
	saving schemes with periodic income	10%
	real estate on rent	
	short term debt funds	
	monthly income plans	15%
	long term	
	provident fund	
	contributory pension schemes	20%
	small savings schemes	
	real estate for own usage	25%
	fixed term deposits	
	jewellery	
	TOTAL SAFETY	*70%*
Yield Enhancing		
	stocks-direct & stock funds	15%
	real estate for investment	5%
	bonds & bond funds	
	Pension ULIPs & others	
	commodities	
	art, antique	
	structured products	
	TOTAL YIELD ENHANCING	*20%*
TOTAL ASSETS		*100%*

SCENARIO 12—*About to retire person, stock market showing deep correction*

55–65 years, personal and economic conditions remain unchanged
P/E at 9, GDP at 8%, earnings growth at 20%, low inflation and interest rates at 5%

ASSET ALLOCATION		
Liquidity	*6–12 mths basic expense*	allocation %
	short term deposits	10%
	liquid funds	
	TOTAL LIQUIDITY	10%
Safety	*current income generating*	
	bonds with coupon	
	saving schemes with periodic income	5%
	real estate on rent	
	short term debt funds	
	monthly income plans	10%
	long term	
	provident fund	
	contributory pension schemes	20%
	small savings schemes	
	real estate for own usage	25%
	fixed term deposits	
	jewellery	
	TOTAL SAFETY	60%
Yield Enhancing		
	stocks-direct & stock funds	25%
	real estate for investment	5%
	bonds & bond funds	
	Pension ULIPs & others	
	commodities	
	art, antique	
	structured products	
	TOTAL YIELD ENHANCING	30%
TOTAL ASSETS		100%

SCENARIO 13—*About to retire person, not so favourable economic conditions*

55–65 years, oil prices are higher, personal conditions same
P/E at 22, GDP at 7%, earnings growth at 12%, medium inflation and interest rates at 9%

ASSET ALLOCATION

Liquidity	*6–12 mths basic expense*	allocation %
	short term deposits	10%
	liquid funds	
	TOTAL LIQUIDITY	*10%*
Safety	*current income generating*	
	bonds with coupon	5%
	saving schemes with periodic income	20%
	real estate on rent	
	short term debt funds	
	monthly income plans	5%
	long term	
	provident fund	
	contributory pension schemes	25%
	small savings schemes	
	real estate for own usage	25%
	fixed term deposits	
	jewellery	
	TOTAL SAFETY	*80%*
Yield Enhancing		
	stocks-direct & stock funds	5%
	real estate for investment	
	bonds & bond funds	5%
	Pension ULIPs & others	
	commodities	
	art, antique	
	structured products	
	TOTAL Yield Enhancing	*10%*
TOTAL ASSETS		*100%*

Stage 5 Above 65 years, retired person, Wealth Harvester

Scenario 14

At this stage, the innings is coming to an end with tail-enders in the fray. They just have to milk the bowling. Active income is completely replaced by passive income. However, some money is still allocated to stocks since the returns there will be very beneficial for leading a long, active and productive post-retirement life.

Scenario 15

Rahul at this stage is still very receptive to new ideas. He wants to nurture new talent. He discovers that new structured products have been introduced in the form of variable retirement annuity products. These give a guaranteed minimum return and in addition are linked to the performance of Sensex.

For example, in a year when Sensex goes down, the investor is guaranteed a return of 5%. But if Sensex goes up by 20 %, he gets an equivalent return of 20%. This enables his participation in prosperous times. His safety needs have not compromised his good and rollicking times even at this stage of his life.

SCENARIO 14—Retired person, wealth harvestor

>65 years, utilizing passive income completely

P/E at 12, GDP at 8%, earnings growth at 20%, low inflation and interest rates at 5%

ASSET ALLOCATION		
Liquidity	*6–12 mths basic expense*	allocation %
	short term deposits	10%
	liquid funds	
	TOTAL LIQUIDITY	10%
Safety	*current income generating*	
	bonds with coupon	5%
	saving schemes with periodic income	25%
	real estate on rent	
	short term debt funds	
	monthly income plans	20%
	long term	
	provident fund	
	contributory pension schemes	
	small savings schemes	
	real estate for own usage	25%
	fixed term deposits	
	jewellery	
	TOTAL SAFETY	75%
Yield Enhancing		
	stocks-direct & stock funds	15%
	real estate for investment	
	bonds & bond funds	
	Pension ULIPs & others	
	commodities	
	art, antique	
	structured products	
	TOTAL YIELD ENHANCING	15%
TOTAL ASSETS		**100%**

SCENARIO 15—Retired person, new exciting retirement annuities but difficult economic conditions

>65 years, retired but still receptive to new talent

P/E at 22, GDP at 7%, earnings growth at 12%, medium inflation and interest rates at 9%

ASSET ALLOCATION		
Liquidity	*6–12 mths basic expense*	allocation %
	short term deposits	10%
	liquid funds	
	TOTAL LIQUIDITY	10%
Safety	*current income generating*	
	bonds with coupon	5%
	saving schemes with periodic income	25%
	real estate on rent	
	short term debt funds	
	monthly income plans	10%
	long term	
	provident fund	
	contributory pension schemes	
	small savings schemes	
	real estate for own usage	25%
	fixed term deposits	
	jewellery	
	TOTAL SAFETY	65%
Yield Enhancing		
	stocks-direct & stock funds	5%
	real estate for investment	
	bonds & bond funds	
	Pension ULIPs & others	
	commodities	
	art, antique	
	structured products	20%
	TOTAL Yield Enhancing	25%
TOTAL ASSETS		100%

Conclusion - The Winning Stroke

Rahul hits the winning stroke and his elation is tremendous on winning the most important game of life. He is coming back to the pavilion – the upright stance, shoulders back, head held high, eyes shining with the intense satisfaction from a very successful tenure at the helm.

He reflects happily on his exhilarating and fulfilling life. He maintained a very good life style and at the same time managed to achieve all his major financial goals. He is very comfortable in the tranquility and serenity of his lovely home. It is in a nice neighbourhood of his choice where good planning facilitated being near his close friends. His children and grandchildren visit him frequently. He feels tremendous joy in the fact that they are well settled, primarily because of the good education he could provide them.

He has complete peace of mind in his harmonious environment. He has the financial freedom to do what he wants. He is closely engaged with community work including mentoring children for achieving their swadharma. He also has the wherewithal to make his retirement even more stimulating and interesting by traveling, taking vacations with his grandchildren, pursuing exotic hobbies or whatever catches his fancy.

The clapping grows into a rising crescendo. The crowd is tremendously excited. They have finally managed to swarm the field and are all around him. He is truly amazed that these results have been achieved by making some very simple and eminently implementable steps. Benefits of playing the wealth game have been truly disproportionate. He looks at the diverse faces in the crowd and conveys with total conviction that all of us can win this one.

www.ingramcontent.com/pod-product-compliance
Lightning Source LLC
Chambersburg PA
CBHW020240250926
51848CB00007BA/511
* 9 7 8 9 3 6 0 7 0 9 7 4 7 *